Clinical Documentation

An Essential Guide for Long-Term Care Nurses

Barbara Acello, MS, RN

HCPro

Clinical Documentation: An Essential Guide for Long-Term Care Nurses is published by HCPro, Inc.

 5 4 3 2 1

ISBN 978-1-57839-950-5

HCPro, Inc., provides information resources for the healthcare industry.

Barbara Acello, MS, RN, Author
Elizabeth Petersen, Senior Managing Editor
Noelle Shough, Executive Editor
Emily Sheahan, Group Publisher
Jean St. Pierre, Director of Operations
Patrick Campagnone, Cover Designer
Michael Roberto, Layout Artist

Arrangements can be made for quantity discounts. For more information, contact:

HCPro, Inc.
P.O. Box 1168
Marblehead, MA 01945
Telephone: 800/650-6787 or 781/639-1872
Fax: 781/639-2982
E-mail: *customerservice@hcpro.com*

Visit HCPro at its World Wide Web sites:
www.hcmarketplace.com* and *www.hcpro.com

1/2007
21064

Contents

Introduction

Section I - Assessment and documentation guidelines *by system*

Section II - Assessment and documentation guidelines *by condition*

Section VI - Resources

Purpose

Long-term care facilities must ensure that their documentation reflects nursing processes and reveals that residents receive care that meets minimum acceptable standards of practice. Each resident's clinical record must be accurate and complete: Evidence of resident assessment, staff interventions, and the resident's response to treatment must be documented. Special procedures performed for the resident's safety and well-being must also be documented. Omissions in documentation suggest that basic, rudimentary care was not provided or that physician orders were not followed. If the accuracy of the clinical record is questionable, other healthcare providers cannot depend on the data to assess and manage the resident's problems—and in a court of law, the chart certainly will not support the argument that your facility provided adequate care.

Nurses cannot choose between giving care and keeping records. Medical records and documentation are part of the care we give as well as validation that conscientious care was delivered. Your documentation must follow the requirements of your state's nurse practice act. The adage "If it wasn't documented, it wasn't done" is as valuable today as it was when you learned it in nursing school. In addition to organizing your documentation based on the five steps of the nursing process—assessment, planning, nursing diagnosis, implementation, and evaluation—your charting should leave no question in a reader's mind that you continually and carefully assessed the resident's condition and monitored his or her progress. Not only does this help ensure legal credibility, but it also ensures that your charting is timely, accurate, truthful and appropriate.[1]

Nurses are responsible for regular, ongoing monitoring of residents who have experienced an acute illness, infection, incident, or other unusual event. Any change in condition, no matter how minor, falls into this category. Standards of nursing practice require that nurses conduct a focused assessment of any involved systems based on the nature of a resident's problem at least once each shift. For example, for a resident with upper respiratory infection, the nurse should assess and document a focused respiratory assessment of the eyes, ears, nose, mouth, neck, and lungs.

This book provides nurses with an easy-to-follow guide for focused nursing assessments and documentation of conditions commonly encountered in the long-term care facility. Written in a list format, this guide is a sort of cheat sheet that lists assessments both by system and condition. Paging through the book, readers will find it is composed almost wholly of bulleted lists describing what to assess and document for

- common problems and conditions seen in the nursing home
- system assessments to identify problems

In addition, to help with any "writer's block" when it comes to assessment and documentation, the nursing notes included in this guide offer succinct lists and guidelines to help nurses out.

The guide also contains useful assessment tools and resources for which nurses are accountable but may not have committed to memory. It's an invaluable resource to ensure that assessments and documentation are focused, concise, and thorough.

1. Habel, M. 2003. Document it right. Would your charting stand up to scrutiny? *Nurseweek*. Online. *www.nurseweek.com*. Accessed 7/29/03.

What to document

In long-term care facilities, a complete assessment is not usually performed every shift unless a resident is ill or is being monitored. Policies and state laws vary on the frequency of narrative charting, but for stable residents, this is generally weekly or monthly. Daily care, treatments, and medications are usually documented on flow sheets.

Acute conditions should be monitored every shift until 24 hours after the condition is resolved or according to facility policy. Documentation should reflect the results of this monitoring, as well as nursing interventions taken.

Clinical documentation that contributes to identification and communication of residents' problems, needs, and strengths; monitors their condition on an ongoing basis; and records treatment and response to treatment is a matter of good clinical practice and an expectation of licensed healthcare professionals.[1] Remember the following:

- If your assessment reveals an abnormality, your documentation should describe what nursing action you took. Simply describing an abnormality is inadequate—as is a notation that simply says "will continue to monitor," in most cases. The nursing process and plan of care should guide all your care and documentation. Review the steps in the nursing process. Don't document an abnormal observation without documenting the other steps related to it in the nursing process. For example, don't document "crackles in lungs" without documenting nursing actions, physician notification, resident response, and follow-up evaluation and care.

- If the resident has a potentially painful condition, such as arthritis or a pressure ulcer, document your regular pain assessments and nursing interventions used to relieve pain. Never make statements that the patient is "smiling; does not appear in pain." Always use an appropriate pain assessment tool in your documentation.

- The purpose of monitoring a resident with an acute illness who receives antibiotic therapy is to monitor the condition. Avoid writing notes that state, "No adverse reaction to antibiotic." Although making such a statement is acceptable, it should only be used as part of a more comprehensive entry. Document vital signs, focused system assessment, and other nursing observations related to the condition for which the resident receives the antibiotic. This shows you are aware of and monitoring the problem. For example, write, "Urine clear amber. Resident denies pain and burning on urination."

- Always document any change in condition along with the resident's vital signs, your actions, and your notification of physician, family, or others. If the resident remains unstable as a result of a change in condition, ongoing assessment and documentation are necessary. Regularly document vital signs, neurological checks, and other observations of the resident's condition.

- If a resident falls, has a fever, or has any change in condition, document every shift until 24 hours after the abnormality is resolved. Do focused assessments of the affected body systems. Take vital signs every shift and, if abnormal, more often.

- Document all unusual occurrences, such as falls, wandering, drug reactions, or changes in condition. Document your notifications about these unusual occurrences to physician, family, and others. Also document nursing actions and the resident's response.

- Follow facility policies for completing incident reports, but regardless of whether your facility uses incident reports, nurses are responsible for documenting the details of all unusual incidents and events in residents' medical records. This documentation should include the nature of the event or incident, assessment, care, notifications, and follow-up monitoring.

Care given

- When documenting, remember you are talking about a person. Review the medical record of a resident with a gastrostomy tube, pressure ulcer, or other chronic condition. Does most of the documentation address the condition? If so, staff are not documenting holistically. Address the entire person; the condition is secondary. Use the nursing process.
- Nursing facilities are required to document the resident's care and response to care during the course of his or her stay, and this documentation is expected to chronicle, support, and be consistent with the findings of each MDS assessment. Always keep in mind that government requirements are not the only reason—or even the major reason—for clinical documentation.[2]
- Make sure your care and documentation are consistent with acceptable professional standards of practice, state laws, facility policies and procedures, and the resident's plan of care.
- Record all nursing care given, including the resident's response to treatment.
- Describe teaching, as well as the resident's response and understanding. List specific instructions you've given.
- Document all safety precautions taken to protect the resident. This may be done on a flow sheet. Be specific—for example, stating "fall precautions" does not tell the reader what you did.

- Always document the reason for giving a PRN medication and the resident's response.
- When following a physician's order, always leave a "paper trail"—that is to say, document an assessment of resident, implementation of valid orders, notification of the physician, and outcome.

1. Morris, JN, and Murphy, K, Nonemaker, S. 2002. *Long Term Care Facility Resident Assessment Instrument (RAI) User's Manual*. Des Moines, IA: Briggs Corp.

2. Ibid.

Communication

- Document communication with others regarding the resident.
- If a change in a resident's condition warrants physician notification, communicate essential information in a clear and logical manner that expedites understanding and intervention. Have all essential data available before calling a physician. Be direct and descriptive—paint a word picture for the physician. Document his or her response.
- On weekends or during second and third shifts, you may communicate with an on-call physician instead of the attending. He or she is probably not familiar with the resident. Clearly summarize the resident's background before describing the problem. Document the physician's response.
- Document all your attempts to reach the physician. If you observe significant or serious changes in the resident's condition, do not just chart them—notify the physician. If he or she does not respond, notify the alternate physician, on-call physician, or medical director.
- Document reservations about a physician's orders and action taken. Legally, you must advocate for the residents. If, in your professional judgment, you believe the physician's orders place a resident in jeopardy, intervene and clarify the treatment plan with him or her. If the physician is unresponsive, contact your supervisor and go up the chain of command from there. Document the actions you take to advocate for the resident.

- Document notifications and referrals, such as notifying a social worker about the need for behavioral intervention, or a dietitian about a pressure ulcer, weight loss, or abnormal lab values.
- When obtaining physician orders for medications, get a diagnosis to correspond with the medication. State the reason why the medication is being given. Many medications have multiple uses.
- Be sure that new physician telephone orders are consistent with other information on the chart. For example, you notify a physician about a 10 lb. weight loss for a resident on a planned reduction program. The physician, who may not remember the resident, orders that the resident take Ensure four times a day. Or worse yet, a physician who is not familiar with the resident may order a drug that duplicates existing medication therapy. Make sure you are familiar with the resident's plan of care and his or her medications before calling a physician.

Section I:

Assessment and documentation guidelines *by system*

Guidelines for assessing and documenting acute conditions

Monitor acute conditions every shift until 24 hours after the condition is resolved, or according to facility policy. Documentation should reflect the results of this monitoring, as well as all nursing interventions taken. If an abnormality is documented, a corresponding nursing action should be taken and documented. Avoid writing statements such as "Will continue to monitor." If continued monitoring is warranted, subsequent nurses' notes will document that it has been done within an appropriate time frame, making this vague statement unnecessary.

Initial documentation guidelines for all conditions that require monitoring

Assess and document the following every shift:

- Focused assessment on systems/problems with signs and symptoms of acute illness.
- Identify the resident's actual problems/complaints, if possible.
- Identify conditions that are or may become unstable.
- If the results of an assessment are positive, describe the nursing action taken. Nursing action must be taken on positive assessment findings. Positive assessment results documented without documenting subsequent action make both the nurse and the facility legally vulnerable and place the resident at risk (e.g., an assessment reveals crackles in the lungs; nursing actions: contact healthcare provider, check vital signs, increase fluids to liquefy secretions, encourage coughing and deep breathing, etc.).
- Describe negative findings (e.g., *No chest pain, no cyanosis*).
- Document vital signs. If abnormal, describe the nursing action taken.
- Initiate pulse oximetry.
- Determine whether the abnormal findings are chronic or acute.
- Check for and consider any recent laboratory values.
- Describe the resident's response to treatment. If he or she is on antibiotic therapy, describe the condition for which antibiotics are being administered,

as well as the resident's signs and symptoms related to that condition. Do a focused assessment on the systems involved and document your findings. Although documenting that "*no side effects to antibiotic therapy*" is acceptable, this should not be the sum total of documentation for the shift. Use a flow sheet to document the absence of side effects to antibiotics to support the note that "No side effects noted this shift related to antibiotic therapy."

- Evaluate new medications and side effects, if any.
- Monitor for signs/symptoms of dehydration and inadequate fluid intake (which causes hypovolemia):
  - Consider intake and output (I&O) monitoring as a nursing measure
- Note any other changes from resident's usual condition (i.e., what he or she is like on a normal day).
- Determine whether other residents in the facility are being treated for or have recently experienced the same or similar signs and symptoms.
- Consider whether a relationship exists between a current sign or symptom and a new medication, food, or fluid intake or a change in activities or physical or mental condition, etc.

Mandatory documenting and reporting

The following signs and symptoms may be present to a greater or lesser extent if an abnormality with any body system is present. The presence of any of these conditions warrants initial assessment, reporting to the healthcare provider, documentation of findings and notifications, and ongoing monitoring until the condition is stabilized:

- Pulse rate below 60 or above 100
- Irregular, weak, or bounding pulse

- Blood pressure below 100/60 or above 140/90, unless this is usual for resident
- Blood pressure is inaudible, or pulse is not able to be palpated
- Pain over center, left, or right chest
- Chest pain that radiates to shoulder, neck, jaw, or arm
- Shortness of breath, dyspnea, or any abnormal respirations
- Headache, dizziness, weakness, paralysis, or vomiting
- Cold, blue, gray, cyanotic, or mottled appearance:
    - Blue color of lips, nail beds, mucous membranes
- Cold, blue, numb, or painful feet or hands
- Feeling faint or lightheaded, losing consciousness
- Respiratory rate below 12 or above 20
- Irregular respirations
- Noisy, labored respirations
- Dyspnea, struggling or gasping for breath
- Cheyne-Stokes respirations
- Wheezing
- Retractions
- Blood sugar over 300
- Blood sugar less than 60
- Prothrombin time greater than one and a half times the control value
- Sodium over 147

- BUN over 22
- WBC over 11,000
- Hematocrit greater than three times the hemoglobin value
- Potassium below 3.5 or over 5.0
- Chloride over 107
- Serum creatinine over 30

Cardiovascular conditions

Assess and document the following every shift:

- Vital signs.
  - Pulse description (e.g., regular, irregular, weak, thready, strong, etc.).
- Capillary refill.
- If pulse oximetry was initiated.
- Presence or absence of chest pain. If present, describe onset, duration, location, radiation, and description.
- Lung sounds. If new abnormalities are noted, alert the healthcare provider.
- The resident's color (e.g., pink, pale, gray, etc.).
- Presence or absence of cyanosis.
- Presence or absence of dyspnea.
- The resident's skin temperature and temperature of distal extremities.
- Activity tolerance.
- Oxygen use, times, liter flow, and resident response.
- Presence or absence of cough. If present, describe whether it is productive or nonproductive. If productive, describe the appearance of sputum.
- Presence or absence of distended neck veins.
- Presence or absence of anxiety.

- Presence or absence of diaphoresis.
- Complaints of chest pain, or pain in shoulder, arm, or jaw.
- Presence or absence of weakness, dizziness, or fatigue.
- Presence or absence of indigestion or nausea.
- Complaints of palpitations.
- Complaints of numbness.
- Complaints of headache.
- Complaints of visual disturbances.
- The resident's mental status.
- If pedal edema is present. Describe, measure with tape measure, and record it.
- Signs or symptoms of thrombophlebitis.
- I&O. Assess whether fluid retention or I&O do not balance.
- Observations about the radial pulse. Note whether the radial pulse is
  - strong
  - weak
  - absent
  - equal (=) bilaterally
  - weaker on the right
  - weaker on the left
- Observations about the pedal pulse. Note whether the pedal pulse is
  - strong

- weak
- absent
- equal (=) bilaterally
- weaker on the right
- weaker on the left

• Presence or absence of edema. Note whether it is

- absent
- nonpitting
- pitting (estimate 1+ through 4+ on edema scale)

Note: Also see "Prerenal azotemia and acute renal failure"

Cardiovascular conditions: Essential documentation and healthcare provider notification

Be sure to document the following and notify the healthcare provider:

- Vital signs (for baseline value)
- Abnormal pulse below 60 or above 100
- Blood pressure below 100/60 or above 140/90
- If you are unable to palpate pulse or hear blood pressure
- Chest pain
- Chest pain that radiates to neck, jaw, or arm
- Shortness of breath

- Headache, dizziness, weakness, or vomiting
- Blue or gray appearance/color
- Cold, blue, painful feet or hands
- Shortness of breath, dyspnea, or abnormal respirations

Eye, ear, nose, throat conditions

Assess and document the following every shift:

- Vital signs
- Respiratory status; describe irregularities, patterns, wheezing
- Presence or absence of headache; if present, describe intensity, location, responsiveness, mental status, etc.
- Nasal congestion; if present, describe
- Condition of pharynx and complaints of sore throat; if present, describe
- Presence or absence of cough; if present, describe whether it is productive or nonproductive, as well as the color and character of sputum
- Exudate from eyes, edema of eyelids, complaints of itching, redness, pain, excess tearing, or reddened sclera
- Alterations in vision; if present, describe
- Condition and appearance of tongue, midline position: color or fissures, etc.
- Appearance of gums and oral mucosa (the area between the gums and cheek will stay moist even with a mouth breather unless resident is dehydrated)
- Drainage from ears, hearing alteration, ringing, etc.
- Whether other residents in the facility are being treated for or have recently experienced the same or similar signs and symptoms

Gastrointestinal (GI) system conditions

Assess and document the following:

- Vital signs.
- Whether a relationship exists between other factors and the signs or symptoms currently exhibited by the resident. For example, if the resident complains of nausea and has had vomiting or diarrhea, is there a relationship between the vomiting and medication administration time, initial doses of new medication, time of day, intake of certain foods or fluids, etc.?
- Whether food and fluid intake are normal for the resident.
- New medications, adverse reactions, and side effects, if any.
- Signs/symptoms of dehydration, inadequate fluid intake (which causes hypovolemia):
  - Consider I&O monitoring as a nursing measure
- Any changes from resident's usual condition (i.e., what he or she is like on a normal day).
- Whether other residents in the facility are being treated for or have recently experienced the same or similar signs and symptoms.
- If the resident is on warfarin, the most recent PT and INR, coagulation status, and any signs of internal bleeding.
- Other recent laboratory values, flat plate abdomen, or x-rays, if any

- Sores or ulcers inside the mouth:
  - Note condition of mucous membranes (note that the area between the gums and cheek will stay moist even with a mouth breather *unless resident is dehydrated*)
- Difficulty chewing or swallowing food.
- Whether the abdomen is
  - soft
  - flat
  - distended
  - taut
- Whether bowel sounds are
  - active
  - hyper
  - hypo
  - absent
  - Note quadrant, location
- Unusual or abnormal appearance of bowel movement.
- Jaundice.
- Blood, mucous, or other unusual substances in stool.
- Unusual color of bowel movement.
- Hard stool, difficulty passing stool.
- Unusual color of stool.

- Abdominal distention.
- Complaints of pain, constipation, diarrhea, or bleeding.
- Complaints of cramping.
- Frequent belching, heartburn, or reflux.
- Changes in appetite.
- Excessive thirst.
- Fruity smell to breath.
- Complaints of indigestion or excessive gas.
- Nausea or vomiting.
- Choking.
- Coffee-ground appearance of emesis or stool.
- Diarrhea. Document the number of stools in an eight-hour shift and describe appearance. Your facility should define diarrhea for you to avoid confusion. Some staff believe residents have diarrhea if they have one loose stool. This is incorrect: Diarrhea is multiple loose stools within a predetermined time frame. Make sure you are familiar with and use the same definition as your facility. Your facility might consider the following in its definition:
  - Three or more loose stools within a 24-hour (or other specified) time period
  - A frequent/profuse discharge of loose or fluid evacuations from the intestines
  - A condition characterized by watery stools, increased frequency of stools, or both compared with what is normal for the resident

- Constipation or fecal impaction. Evaluate recent documentation of bowel movements to determine whether it reflects a change from the resident's usual pattern
- Past history of GI problems. Consider such problems as ileus, bowel obstruction, impaction, gastritis, GI bleeding, etc.

Abdomen assessment

Assess and document whether the abdomen is

- soft
- flat
- distended
- taut
- tender or painful (specify location)

Bowel sounds

Assess and document whether bowel sounds are

- active
- hyperactive
- hypoactive
- absent

Note: Also see "Prerenal azotemia and acute renal failure."

GI system infection

If the resident has a GI system infection, assess and document the following:

- Vital signs
- Unusual or abnormal appearance or color of bowel movement
- Blood, mucous, or other unusual substances in stool
- Diarrhea
- Jaundice
- Complaints of indigestion or excessive gas
- Nausea or vomiting
- Abdominal pain
- Whether other residents in the facility are being treated for or have recently experienced the same or similar signs and symptoms

Genitourinary system conditions

Assess and document the following:

- Vital signs
- Urinary output too low
- Oral intake too low
- Fluid I&O not balanced
- Abnormal appearance of urine (e.g., dark, concentrated, red, cloudy)
- Unusual material in urine (e.g., blood, pus, particles)
- Complaints of difficulty urinating
- Complaints of pain, burning, urgency, frequency, or pain in lower back
- Frequent urination in small amounts
- Sudden-onset incontinence
- Edema
- Sudden weight loss or gain
- Respiratory distress
- Change in mental status
- Recent laboratory values, if any
- New medications, adverse reactions, and side effects, if any

- Signs/symptoms of dehydration, inadequate fluid intake (which causes hypovolemia)
  - Consider I&O monitoring

Note: Also see "Prerenal azotemia and acute renal failure."

Genitourinary system infection

If the resident has a genitourinary system infection, assess and document the following:

- Vital signs
- Urinary output too low
- Oral intake too low
- Abnormal appearance of urine (e.g., dark, concentrated, red, or cloudy)
- Change in appearance, color, or odor of urine that does not promptly respond to increased fluids
- Unusual material in urine (e.g., blood, pus, or particles)
- Complaints of pain, burning, urgency, frequency, or pain in lower back
- Foul odor to urine
- Edema
- Sudden weight loss or gain
- Respiratory distress
- Change in mental status
- Unexplained deterioration of physical function
- Change in mental status

- New or worsening cognitive impairment, increasing confusion
- Delirium
- Agitation, restlessness
- Lethargy
- Anorexia
- Decline in mobility
- Falls
- Nonspecific complaints of feeling ill
- New episode of incontinence, increased frequency of incontinence, or nocturia
- Cough
- Nausea or vomiting
- Abdominal pain
- Body language or other behavior suggesting pain
- Whether other residents in the facility are being treated for or have recently experienced the same or similar signs and symptoms

Note: Also see "Prerenal azotemia and acute renal failure."

Hematologic conditions: Anticoagulant therapy

Assess and document the following:

- Vital signs
- Rate and character of pulse
- Capillary refill
- Orthostatic blood pressure
- Presence of tachycardia
- Presence or absence of dyspnea
- Initiate pulse oximetry
- Presence of active bleeding, including blood in urine or stools
- Presence of excessive menstrual bleeding, if not menopausal
- Whether the resident bleeds easily, such as during toothbrushing
- Persistent oozing from superficial injuries
- Bleeding from tumor, ulcer, or skin lesions
- Presence or absence of petechiae or ecchymosis, purpura
- Presence or absence of abdominal distention; if present, measure abdominal girth and check for liver size and tenderness
- Presence of unexplained edema
- Presence or absence of cyanosis

- Presence of jaundice
- Lymph node enlargement, if any
- Signs of anemia, including pale skin color, conjunctiva, mucous membranes, nail beds, and syncope
- Complaints of weakness, dizziness, or fatigue
- Complaints of headache or visual disturbances
- Abnormal sensation, proprioception, or gait
- Complaints of nausea; if vomiting, check for hematemesis
- Dyspnea on exertion
- Complaints of bone pain or headache
- Increasing complaints of pain anywhere in body
- Presence of diaphoresis
- Complaints of palpitations
- Lab values, PT, INR, and others as ordered (monitor, document, and report)

Note: Also see "Prerenal azotemia and acute renal failure."

Integumentary system conditions

- Check vital signs
- If diabetic, note fasting blood glucose reading (fingerstick)
- Determine whether resident has a history of this or other dermatological conditions
- Rash—describe blisters, pustules, scabs, bites, etc.
- Itching (pruritus)—note whether scratches present/absent on skin:
  - Note whether itching is more intense; day or night
- Note complaints of pain (to determine intensity, use the resident's preferred pain scale):
  - Note specific location of pain
- Redness
- Redness in the skin that does not go away within 30 minutes after pressure is relieved
- Scaling or flaking (e.g., in psoriasis or eczema)
- Pressure sores
- Irritation
- Bruises
- Skin discoloration

- Swelling
- Lumps
- Abnormal sweating
- Excessive heat or coolness to touch
- Open areas/skin breakdown
- Drainage
- Foul odor
- Complaints, such as numbness, burning, or tingling
- Signs of infection
- Unusual skin color, such as blue or gray color of the skin, lips, nail beds, roof of mouth, or mucous membranes (also see GI system for jaundice)
- Skin growths
- Poor skin turgor/tenting of skin
- Sunken, dark appearance around eyes
- Note whether skin is
    - warm to touch
    - cool to touch
    - dry
    - clammy
    - diaphoretic, moist
    - color normal or abnormal for resident (describe if abnormal)

  - pale
  - dusky
  - cyanotic
  - jaundiced
  - edematous
  - turgor good, fair, poor

- Note condition of mucous membranes (note that the area between the gums and cheek will stay moist even with a mouth breather *unless resident is dehydrated*)
- Note whether edema is present/absent:
  - No edema present
  - Nonpitting
  - Pitting (estimate 1+ through 4+ on edema scale)

Integumentary system infection

If the resident has an integumentary system infection, assess and document the following:

- Vital signs
- Rash
- Redness
- Swelling
- Open areas/skin breakdown

- Drainage
- Foul odor
- Determine whether other residents in the facility are being treated or have recently experienced the same or similar signs and symptoms

Wound abnormalities

- Vital signs
- Redness near and around the wound
- Exudate, presence or absence of odor and unusual drainage, note if purulent or foul-smelling
    - Type of drainage:
        - Sanguineous—thin, bright red
        - Serosanguineous—thin, watery, pale red to pink
        - Serous—thin, watery, clear
        - Purulent—thick or thin, commonly yellow, but may be opaque tan to yellow
        - Foul purulent—thick opaque yellow to green with offensive odor
    - Amount of drainage:
        - None—wound tissue dry
        - Scant—no measurable drainage, but wound tissue is moist
        - Small—wound tissue is very moist, with drainage on < 25% of the dressing
        - Moderate—wound tissue wet, drainage involves 25 to 75% of the dressing

  - Large—wound tissue filled with fluid and involves > 75% of the dressing
  - Copious—wound tissue saturated and dressing is saturated; may be leaking and does not contain drainage

- Necrotic tissue:
  - Eschar is commonly dark in color and has a thick, hard consistency; note whether loose or adherent
  - Slough is usually lighter in color and has a thin, stringy consistency
- Determine whether granulation tissue is present or absent:
  - Granulation tissue is usually beefy red, granular, or bubbly in appearance
  - Differentiate granulation tissue from a smooth, red wound bed
  - Describe color of tissue (pale pink to dusky red)
- Heat
- Edema
- Increased pain or tenderness
- Fever
- Edema of tissue surrounding the wound
- Separation of wound edges
- Trauma or injury
- Maceration, water-logged appearance of the wound edges
- Bruising
- Frank bleeding

Pressure ulcers: Stages

- *Stage I*—an observable, pressure-related alteration of intact skin, whose indicators as compared to an adjacent or opposite area on the body may include changes in one or more of the following parameters:
  - Skin temperature (warmth or coolness);
  - Tissue consistency (firm or boggy);
  - Sensation (pain, itching)
  - A defined area of persistent redness in lightly pigmented skin, whereas in darker skin tones the ulcer may appear with persistent red, blue, or purple hues

Note: Stage I pressure ulcers may be difficult to identify because they are not readily visible and present with greater variability. Advanced technology (not commonly available in nursing homes) has shown that a Stage I pressure ulcer may have minimal to substantial tissue damage in layers beneath the skin's surface, even when there is no visible surface penetration. The Stage I indicators identified above will generally persist or be evident after the pressure on the area has been removed for 30–45 minutes. If a reddened area blanches, the tissue damage may be irreversible. If the tissue remains blanched for a long time, the likelihood of serious tissue damage and ulcer development is high. Pressure ulcers begin inside the tissue. By the time damage extends to the outside, it may be too late to prevent ulcer development.

- *Stage II*—partial thickness skin loss involving epidermis, dermis, or both. The ulcer is superficial and presents clinically as an abrasion, blister, or shallow crater.

- *Stage III*—full-thickness skin loss involving damage to, or necrosis of, subcutaneous tissue that may extend down to, but not through, underlying fascia. The ulcer presents clinically as a deep crater with or without undermining of adjacent tissue.
- *Stage IV*—full-thickness skin loss with extensive destruction; tissue necrosis; or damage to muscle, bone, or supporting structures (e.g., tendon, joint capsule). Undermining and sinus tracts also may be associated with Stage IV pressure ulcers.

Pressure ulcers: Assessment and documentation

Assess and document the following weekly, any time a change occurs, upon discharge or pass, or according to facility policy:

- Careful documentation is essential. Avoid subjective comments, such as "healing well" in pressure ulcer documentation. Document what you see.
- Measure and document the length, width, and depth in centimeters. Use a head-to-toe axis for length and a hip-to-hip axis for width. If the wound is large or irregularly shaped, document that the measurements were taken at the longest and widest parts of the wound. Draw a picture of the wound and mark its features and measurements in your notes. Measure depth at the deepest point in the wound bed. Note tunneling, using a clock to describe tunnel locations.
- Assess and document the appearance of the wound. Begin at the center and work outward. If the wound is various colors, describe them by using percentages, such as 80% red and 20% black. This is helpful if you cannot identify the red tissue. Granulation tissue is usually beefy red, granular, or bubbly in appearance. Exposed muscle has a smooth surface and is pink to red. Slough

is usually lighter in color and has a thin, stringy consistency; it is commonly yellow, tan, or gray in color. Eschar is black or dark brown, but is occasionally deep red; it is often thick and leathery in appearance. Also, identify undermining, tunnels, and sinus tracts within the wound bed. Tunnels are larger and easily observed; sinus tracts are small, with a narrower opening. Undermining is sometimes called "rimming" and means that the wound margins seem loose and overhang the ulcer bed. The overhanging area often involves a significant Part of the wound edge. This may be due to infection with streptococci or another bacteria. The tissue destruction extends underneath the intact skin around the wound margins. Undermining is often seen in injuries caused by friction and shearing, particularly in sacral ulcers.

- Assess and document the edges of the wound. Note whether they are well defined or diffuse, macerated; if the edges have rolled under; if there is new skin growth; or undermining. Check for scarring, callus formation (hyperkeratosis), and dry scaling.
- Assess and document the color, odor, amount, consistency, and nature of wound drainage (exudate).
- Note and document the appearance and temperature of the periwound skin. Monitor for signs of infection, such as erythema, edema, induration, warmth, cellulitis, crepitus, maceration, and damage such as skin tears or abrasions from previous dressings.
- Document regular pain assessments and medication administered for pain relief, including resident response.

Musculoskeletal conditions: Fractures

If the resident has a musculoskeletal condition or fracture, assess and document the following:

- Vital signs
- Pain
- Obvious deformity
- Immobility
- Inability to move arms/legs
- Inability to move one or more joints
- Limited/abnormal range of motion
- Jerking or shaky movements
- Weakness
- Sensory changes
- Changes in the ability to sit, stand, move, or walk
- Pain upon movement
- Description of fracture site, edema or other abnormality
- Presence or absence of edema
- Skin—open or intact; describe

- If cast, appearance of extremity distal to cast (describe pain, pallor [color], presence or absence of pulse, ability to move extremity)
- Skin temperature distal to cast
- Sensation in the affected area
- Presence or absence of bleeding, if surgical site or open fracture
- Tachycardia, hypotension, and signs of shock
- Signs of fat embolism, including decreased mental acuity, respiratory rate, chest pain, dyspnea
- Complaints of pain
- Range of motion
- Bed mobility; number of assistants
- Ability to transfer and bear weight, if any; number of assistants
- Activity tolerance
- What the resident can and cannot do without staff assistance
- Assistive devices, if any, for bed mobility and out-of-bed activities

Neurological conditions

Assess and document the following:

- Vital signs
- Neurological assessment; deteriorating level of consciousness is the most important indication of neurological problems
- Increasing mental confusion
- Initiate pulse oximetry
- Capillary refill
- Loss of sensation
- Numbness, tingling
- Change in pupil size; unequal pupils
- Abnormal or involuntary motor function
- Loss of ability to move a body part
- Incoordination
- Progressive drowsiness, sleepiness for no apparent reason, progressive lethargy
- Response to stimuli
- Hand grip strength
- If head injury, neurological checks for at least 72 hours

- If suspected CVA, Glasgow Coma Scale, Cincinnati Stroke Scale, ABCD Stroke Scale
- Pupil checks
- Complaints of headache
- Complaints of visual disturbances
- Strength, balance, paresthesia
- Presence or absence of
  - paralysis
  - emotional lability
  - dysphagia
  - speech difficulty
  - tremors; if present, describe if fine or coarse
- Bowel and bladder function
- Presence or absence of contractures
- Presence or absence of pressure ulcers
- Bed mobility; number of assistants
- Ability to transfer and bear weight, if any; number of assistants
- Activity tolerance
- What the resident can and cannot do without staff assistance
- Assistive devices, if any, for bed mobility and out-of-bed activities
- Presence of pain; describe assessment and nursing intervention

- Impairment, if any—loss of sensation and reflexes
- Dependent edema, if any, and nursing interventions
- Presence of seizure activity, if any
- Rehabilitation documentation—ensure that nursing documentation does not contradict it; for example, if rehab states "resident transfers with one minimum assist," nursing documentation should be consistent—it shouldn't say, "two maximum assistants."

Mental status

Assess and document the following:

- Change in level of consciousness, orientation, awareness, or alertness
- Changes in mood or behavior
- Change in ability to express self or communicate
- Excessive drowsiness
- Sleepiness for no apparent reason
- Sudden onset of mental confusion
- Threats of harm to self or others
- Sensorium/oriented to
    - time
    - place
    - person
    - season

Mental status problems related to infection

If the resident has mental status problems related to infection, assess and document the following:

- Change in level of consciousness, orientation, awareness, or alertness
- Changes in mood or behavior
- Change in ability to express self or communicate
- Mental confusion, clouding of sensorium
- Severe headache
- Visual disturbances
- New medications and side effects, if any
- Signs/symptoms of dehydration or inadequate fluid intake (which causes hypovolemia):
  - Consider I&O monitoring
- Other recent laboratory values, if any
- Any other changes from resident's usual condition (i.e., what he or she is like on a normal day)
- Determine whether other residents in the facility are being treated for or have recently experienced the same or similar signs and symptoms

Mental status related to new medication

To determine whether the resident has mental status problems related to new medication, assess using the mnemonic **ACUTE CHANGE IN MS**:

INITIAL	DRUG CLASS
A	Antiparkinson agents
C	Corticosteroids
U	Urinary incontinence agents
T	Theophylline
E	Emptying drugs (drugs that stimulate upper GI motility)
C	Cardiovascular drugs
H	H2 blockers
A	Antimicrobials
N	NSAIDs
G	Geropsychiatric drugs
E	ENT drugs
I	Insomnia drugs
N	Narcotics
M	Muscle relaxants
S	Seizure drugs

Although we know that certain drugs and drug categories are likely to cause cognitive changes, polypharmacy is also an important consideration. The American Nurses Association supports the safe and effective use of drug therapy for older adults resulting from collaborative efforts of those who prescribe, those who administer, and the older adults who take the drugs. In any event, they advise that a judicious approach to medication administration should be used with elderly individuals.[1]

1. American Nurses Association, eds. 1997. Position statement on polypharmacy in the older adult. Online. *www.nursingworld.org*.

Pulse check

Normal pulse ranges from approximately 60 BPM–100 BPM, but this can vary by about 10%. The following clinical presentations may indicate an acute condition change and should be assessed further:

- Sustained change from normal range
- Change in usual pulse rhythm or regularity
- Pulse > 120 BPM or < 50 BPM (use facility criteria; many facilities use > 100 BPM or < 60 BPM)
- Pulse > 100 BPM combined with other symptoms (e.g., palpitations, dyspnea, or dizziness)

Note whether pulses are

- strong
- weak
- absent
- equal (=) bilaterally
- > on right
- > on left

Pulse assessment:

- Peripheral: identify pulse rhythm, volume, and rate
- Apical: listen with the diaphragm of stethoscope

Locate apex of heart, usually at the left 5th intercostal at the midclavicular line:

- Note strength and regularity of rhythm
- Count rate (count one full minute if the rhythm is irregular)

Pulse oximetry values

Pulse oximeter reading	Interpretation
95%–100%	Normal
Below 90%	Suggests complications, impending hypoxemia
85%	Inadequate oxygen for body function, condition worsening, potential impending crisis
Below 70%	Life-threatening

- If abnormal values noted, document your focused assessment of the resident's condition at the time the abnormal value is noted

Signs and symptoms of decreased ability to ventilate are as follows:

- Anxiety.
- Restlessness.
- Capillary refill > three seconds.
- Cyanosis.
- Dyspnea.
- Tachypnea.
- Decreased level of consciousness.
- Increased work of breathing.

- Decreasing ability to protect airway.
- Monitor the resident, not the machine; if the unit shows life-threatening values but the resident is in no distress, reconcile the problem. Document focused assessment and vital signs.

Respiratory system conditions

- Vital signs
- Respiratory rate below 12 or above 20
- Capillary refill
- Initiate pulse oximetry
- Slow, rapid, gasping, deep, shallow, or irregular respirations
- Noisy, labored respirations
- Dyspnea, shortness of breath
- Gasping for breath
- Cheyne-Stokes respirations
- Wheezing
- Coughing
  - Productive or nonproductive; if productive, describe color and amount of sputum
- Nasal discharge present/absent
- Resident's skin, lips, tongue, ear lobes, mucous membranes, or nail beds are cyanotic:
  - Resident's overall skin appearance has blue, gray, mottled appearance

- Changes in mental status, including decreased responsiveness, drowsiness, sleepiness for no apparent reason, restlessness, progressively increasing confusion
- Tachycardia
- Any abnormal lung sounds noted:
    - Clear on right, anterior or posterior
    - Clear on left, anterior or posterior
    - Coarse
    - Wheezes
    - Rales (crackles)
    - Rhonchi
- Movement in the chest is absent, minimal, or irregular
- Breathing movement appears to be in the abdomen, not the lungs
- Air movement cannot be detected by listening and feeling for breath sounds on your cheek and ear
- Resident is unable to speak at all, or cannot speak in sentences because he or she is short of breath
- Nasal flaring is present during inspiration
- The muscles below the ribs/above the clavicles retract inward during respiration
- Evaluate resident's past history of other respiratory conditions or related problems, such as CHF or COPD

Lung check

- Clear right, anterior or posterior
- Clear left, anterior or posterior
- Coarse
- Wheezes
- Rales (crackles)
- Respirations:
    - Normal breathing is effortless, quiet, and regular
    - Count rate and depth
- Breathing patterns
    - Eupnea
    - Cheyne-Stokes
    - Cluster breathing
    - Hyperventilation

Respiratory system infection

- Vital signs
- Capillary refill
- Initiate pulse oximetry
- Fever > 101°F
- Rapid respirations
- Irregular respirations

- Noisy, labored respirations
- Dyspnea
- Coughing, nasal drainage
- Blue color of lips or nail beds, mucous membranes
- Determine whether other residents in the facility are being treated for or have recently experienced the same or similar signs and symptoms

Skin check

- Warm to touch
- Cool to touch
- Dry
- Clammy
- Diaphoretic, moist
- Color normal
- Pale
- Dusky
- Cyanotic
- Jaundiced
- Turgor (good, fair, poor)—note location checked
- Mucous membranes for moisture (note that the area between the gums and cheek will stay moist even with a mouth breather unless resident is dehydrated)

Vital signs suggesting an acute change in condition

Temperature

- A range of 98.2°F (36.8°C) to 99.9°F (37.7°C) oral temperature is considered normal. A resident's normal temperature will vary by up to 0.9°F (0.5°C) daily.
- Try to establish the resident's normal temperature range as soon as possible after admission. This can be readily done if regular admission monitoring includes vital signs. Consider taking vital signs every shift (or more often if abnormal) during this assessment period.
- A sudden or rapid change from normal temperature may suggest an acute change of condition. One temperature reading above 100°F, two readings above 99°F, or an increase of 2°F above the upper end of the resident's normal range may be a positive sign of an acute condition change.
- After an isolated temperature reading that is outside the resident's normal range, repeat temperature readings approximately every four hours for 24 hours and assess for other signs and symptoms to determine whether an acute change of condition exists.
- Hypothermia may also indicate a possible acute change of condition. Subnormal temperatures often indicate acute illness, sepsis, or shock in elderly persons. Never ignore this important diagnostic sign!
- An electric thermometer is the preferred method for taking temperature. Avoid the axillary method unless other methods are contraindicated.

If a tympanic thermometer is used, make sure the lens is inserted correctly and is flat against the eardrum.

- Assess the resident for factors that may affect temperature, such as medications.

Pulse

Normal pulse ranges from approximately 60 BPM–100 BPM, but this can vary by about 10%. The following clinical presentations may indicate an acute condition change and should be assessed further:

- Sustained change from normal range
- Change in usual pulse rhythm or regularity
- Pulse > 120 BPM or < 50 BPM (use facility criteria; many facilities use > 100 or < 60)
- Pulse > 100 BPM combined with other symptoms (e.g., palpitations, dyspnea, or dizziness)

Respirations

- Respiratory rates > 28 breaths/min (normal in younger adults is 12–15 breaths/min; in the elderly, 16–25 breaths/min, with approximate 2:1 inspiration/expiration ratio)
- Marked change from usual respiration pattern or rhythm
- Irregular breathing, long pauses between breaths, audible noises related to breathing
- Struggling to breathe (e.g., gasping for breath, using accessory muscles of the neck)

- Pulse oximetry values below 90
- Capillary refill > three seconds

Blood pressure

- Try to establish the resident's usual blood pressure (BP) range as soon as possible after admission. This can be readily done if regular admission monitoring includes vital signs. Consider taking vital signs every shift (or more often if abnormal) during this assessment period (Normal range is approximately systolic 100 mmHg–140 mmHg, diastolic 60 mmHg–90 mmHg). Note that new criteria were released in 2003 that further divide the normal category. For additional information, go to *www.nhlbi.nih.gov/hbp/*.
- A change in BP is more often a symptom than a cause of an acute change of condition. Isolated BP elevations generally are not significant. Sustained elevations in systolic pressure should trigger further assessment. A BP change alone should not trigger a call to the practitioner without additional signs or symptoms (e.g., sustained elevation, new neurological symptoms).
- A decrease in systolic BP > 120 mmHg when moving from a prone to a seated position or from a standing position signals orthostatic hypotension. This condition is a great contributing risk factor for falls and is often overlooked. Consult the healthcare provider if you've identified this condition. Note this on the care plan and fall risk documentation.
- Any significant decrease in BP may signal an acute change of condition (e.g., systolic BP < 100 mmHg if baseline is 110 mmHg, decline in BP accompanied by other symptoms such as dizziness, decline > 15 mm in systolic BP, combination of pulse > 100 beats per minute [BPM]/systolic BP < 100 mmHg).

General guidelines for abnormal vital sign reporting

- If the resident is symptomatic, follow the guidelines for immediate reporting. Use good nursing judgment when determining whether to report immediately or wait until the next business day.
- All vital signs in the immediate and next day reporting categories must be monitored every four hours or as ordered until they have been stable for 72 hours.

Guidelines for immediate reporting

- Systolic BP > 210 mmHg, < 90 mmHg
- Diastolic BP > 115 mmHg
- Resting pulse > 130 bpm, < 55 bpm, or > 110 bpm, and patient has dyspnea or palpitations
- Respirations > 28, < 10/minute
- Oral (electronic thermometer) temperature > 101°F
- Oral (electronic thermometer) temperature < 96°F

Guidelines for reporting next business day

- Diastolic BP routinely > 90 mmHg
- Resting pulse > 120 bpm on repeat exam
- Oral (electronic thermometer) temperature > 100°F
- Oral (electronic thermometer) temperature < 97°F

Section II:

Assessment and documentation guidelines *by condition*

24-hour change of condition

The resident "just isn't right," but nursing personnel are unsure about the problem. Before contacting the healthcare provider, be prepared to report the following:

- Current vital signs
- Capillary refill
- Initiate pulse oximetry
- Current height and weight
- Recent lab or x-ray findings, if any
- Resident's past history of these or similar symptoms
- Whether the resident is on dialysis
- Whether the resident is on anticoagulants (e.g., warfarin). If yes, note the
  - most recent PT and INR values and date
  - daily dosage of drug
- Onset of signs and symptoms:
  - What are signs and symptoms?
  - When did they begin?
- Resident's activity, behavior, and mental status over the past few days
- Resident's last bowel movement
- Resident's food and fluid intake over the past few days

- Fingerstick blood sugar, if resident is diabetic
- If neurological signs and symptoms are present, note Glasgow Coma Scale, Cincinnati Stroke Scale, ABCD Stroke Scale if neurological signs and symptoms
- Pupil reaction and neurological state, if applicable
- Resident's usual medications
  - Any new medications?

Assess and document the following each shift:

- Vital signs.
- Special monitoring, such as I&O, pulse oximeter and neurological checks, Glasgow Coma Scale.
- Focused assessment of affected system.
- Healthcare provider, resident, family notification:
  - Their response
- Nursing care and resident response.
- Religious considerations met, if indicated.
- Follow-up at 24 to 72 hours.
- Care plan, nursing care instructions updated.
- Recent laboratory values, if any.
- New medications and side effects, if any.
- Any changes from resident's usual condition (i.e., what he or she is like on a normal day).

- Whether other residents in the facility are being treated for or have recently experienced the same or similar signs and symptoms.
- Whether a relationship exists between the other factors and signs or symptoms the resident currently exhibits and other factors. For example, if the resident complains of nausea and has had vomiting or diarrhea, is there a relationship between the vomiting and medication administration time, initial doses of new medication, time of day, intake of certain foods or fluids, etc.?

Acute pulmonary infection: Acute exacerbation COPD

Assess and document the following each shift:

- Vital signs
- Pulse oximetry
- Capillary refill
- Lung sounds:
  - If new abnormalities are noted, is healthcare provider aware?
- Respiratory pattern, including rate, rhythm, effort, and use of accessory muscles
- The resident's color (e.g., pink, pale, gray, etc.)
- Presence or absence of cyanosis
- Presence or absence of dyspnea
  - If present, describe whether at rest, upon exertion, etc.
- Presence or absence of cough. If present,
  - note whether it's new, chronic, or exacerbated
  - describe whether it's productive or nonproductive; if productive, describe appearance of sputum
- Activity tolerance
- Oxygen use, times, liter flow, resident response

- Presence or absence of chest pain
- Presence of distended neck veins
- Presence or absence of anxiety
- Presence or absence of diaphoresis
- Complaints of pain
- Presence or absence of weakness, dizziness, fatigue, or malaise
- Mental status and level of consciousness
- Presence or absence of pedal edema; if present, describe
- Anorexia, weight loss

Anticoagulant drug therapy

- Question the resident's healthcare provider about the need for regular monitoring and frequency of protime and INR. For monitoring, do the following:
  - Schedule labs
  - Notify healthcare provider about *abnormal* values immediately
  - Notify healthcare provider no later than the next business day about *normal* lab values
- Document teaching to the resident, responsible party, and staff about the following:
  - Potential drug and medical condition interactions
  - Drug side effects
  - Drug-food interactions
  - Complications
  - Need for laboratory monitoring
  - Issues to report related to anticoagulant therapy
- Monitor for and document daily (documentation may be managed by using a flow sheet):
  - Blood in the urine
  - Abdominal or flank pain
  - Dark, tarry stools or frank bleeding in the stool

- Blood in emesis, bloody nose, or coughing up blood
- Bleeding gums
- Nosebleed
- Bruising
- Hematoma
- Pain in joints and joint immobility
- Neurologic changes
- Interactions with food or other medications that potentiate or inhibit anticoagulation
- Increased pain
- Fever
- Loss of appetite, nausea, vomiting, abdominal cramping, and rash
- Signs of skin necrosis
- Your communications with others, including dietitian, pharmacist, lab, healthcare provider
- Notifications of abnormal labs and actions taken

• Document/describe nursing actions and intervention:

- Describe the resident's response to nursing intervention
- Document notifications of healthcare provider and responsible parties

- Initiate and document your request for the following:
  - A dietary evaluation for drug/food interactions
  - A pharmacist evaluation for drug/drug interactions
  - 24-hour monitoring any time labs are abnormal

Autonomic dysreflexia

Definition

Autonomic dysreflexia is a potentially life-threatening complication of spinal cord injury. It usually occurs in residents with injuries above the midthoracic area or the sixth thoracic vertebra. As a rule, injuries that would normally cause pain below the level of the spinal damage set this chain of events in motion. Any irritation can trigger this condition (*including very minor irritants*), but the most common cause is a full bladder. Other common problems are a full rectum or something pinching the skin. The signs and symptoms indicate uncontrolled sympathetic nervous system activity. The irritation triggers a reflex reaction that markedly increases blood pressure. The pulse also increases and may become irregular. Because the nerves in the spinal cord are damaged, they cannot correct or control the situation. The remedy is to quickly identify the cause and return the blood pressure to normal. Although the resident may recognize the onset of symptoms, he or she has no way of knowing what is causing the blood pressure elevation. People with spinal cord injury often describe this condition with the phrase "going hyper."

Treatment for this condition involves rapidly identifying the offending stimulus and removing it. Nurses who work with residents with spinal cord injury must be able to recognize autonomic dysreflexia quickly and take appropriate nursing action. Become familiar with your residents' average blood pressures. People with spinal cord injury often have normal or low blood pressure. An increase in blood pressure of 20 mmHg suggests the onset of symptoms. Undetected, the blood pressure will continue to rise to dangerously high levels. The outcome of this condition is largely determined by how quickly personnel identify it.

Causative factors

The most common causes of autonomic dysreflexia are bladder problems, such as the following:

- Overfull bladder (this is the most common cause)
- Irritation of the bladder wall
- Urinary retention
- Urinary infection
- Blocked catheter
- Noncompliance with intermittent catheterization schedule
- Overfilled urinary drainage bag or leg bag

Other less common potential causes include the following:

- Constipation or fecal impaction
- Hemorrhoids
- Infection or irritation in the abdomen, such as appendicitis or acute abdominal conditions
- Pressure ulcers
- Prolonged pressure—such as by an object in the chair or shoe, sitting on wrinkled clothing, etc.
- Minor injury, such as a cut, bruise, or abrasion
- Ingrown toenails
- Burns, including sunburn

- Pressure on or pinching of skin from tight or constrictive clothing
- Menstrual cramps
- Labor and delivery
- Overstimulation during sexual activity
- Fractured bones
- Gas (indigestion)

Signs and symptoms

Document all of the following signs and symptoms, if present:

- Extremely high blood pressure (may be as high as 200/100)
- Severe headache
- Red, flushed face
- Red blotches on the skin above the level of spinal injury
- Sweating above the level of spinal injury
- Stuffy nose
- Nausea
- Bradycardia
- Blurry vision, seeing spots, or any other visual disturbances
- Goose bumps below the level of injury
- Chills without fever
- Cold, clammy skin below the level of injury

Nursing actions

Perform and document the following nursing actions:

- Elevate the head of the bed to high Fowler's position, or as high as tolerated.
- Lower the legs.
- Quickly troubleshoot the bladder.
- Because problems related to catheters are among the most common causes of this condition, first check the catheter and drainage bag for problems and determine whether a catheter change is warranted (consider changing the catheter if the drainage bag contains a large amount of sediment).
- If no catheter is in place, the healthcare provider may order insertion. Consider using Lidocaine gel instead of water-soluble lubricant.
- If the resident is on an intermittent catheterization schedule, do a straight catheterization immediately to empty the bladder.
- When inserting a catheter for a resident with this condition, empty the bladder slowly. Rapid drainage may worsen the condition by causing bladder spasms.
- Notify the healthcare provider promptly.
- Make sure tubing is positioned correctly and that urine is not refluxing into the bladder.
- Remove kinks or obstructions in tubing, if present.
- Empty the leg bag or urinary drainage bag.
- Irrigate using a small volume (15 mL) of room-temperature solution once. A cold solution may worsen the condition.

- Use nursing judgment regarding benefits vs. risks of removing appliances such as ace wraps, binders, or antiembolism hosiery.
- Remove tight and constricting clothing, shoes, and appliances, if appropriate.
- Monitor blood pressure every two to three minutes.
- Avoid movements or activities that would cause the resident to bear down as if having a bowel movement. Bearing down has the potential to worsen the syndrome.
- Be calm and reassuring. This condition is frightening for the resident.
- Problems related to the bowel are the second most likely cause of autonomic dysreflexia. If no bladder-related problems are noted, do the following:
  - Check for a fecal impaction. If found, remove it carefully. Use an anesthetic lubricating jelly instead of water-soluble lubricant. Instill the jelly into the rectum to numb the mucous membranes, then wait about two to five minutes for it to take effect.
- Skin-related problems are the third most likely cause of autonomic dysreflexia. If no bowel problems are identified, do the following:
  - Undress and reposition the resident and carefully check the entire body for pressure ulcers and other problems, such as ingrown toenails.
- When the offending stimulus has been identified and treated, monitor the resident for rebound hypotension. This condition is most likely to occur if the blood pressure was lowered by giving medications. (Medications are not usually necessary if the noxious causative stimulus is identified and eliminated.)

- Continue to monitor the blood pressure every five minutes after the episode is completely resolved.
- Monitoring frequency will vary from every five minutes to every 30 minutes, depending on the resident's baseline condition and response to treatment.
- Keep the healthcare provider apprised of the resident's blood pressure.

Note: Residents who have experienced autonomic dysreflexia are always at risk for a recurrence. Prevention is the preferred treatment goal, so the care plan should be modified promptly to emphasize preventive care.

Behavior change

Assess and document the following each shift:

- Vital signs
- Precipitating factor(s), if known
- Consideration of a trigger to the behavior
- Description of change compared with normal
- Whether there is a pattern or cycle to the behavior
- Nonpharmacological interventions that have been effective in diverting or reducing the behavior
- The physical assessment, which includes the following:
  - Evaluation for signs and symptoms of physical illness, including UTI
  - Review of recent labs; if none present, discuss the need for them with healthcare provider
  - Vital signs
  - Neuro check
  - Glasgow Coma Scale
  - Other, as indicated
- Consideration given to transfer or relocation shock, change in life or family situation, etc.
  - Use the Holmes-Rahe Social Adjustment Rating Scale, if indicated

- Note
  - any behavior changes, including a description of the behavior and cause, if known
  - any mood changes, relationship difficulties
  - personal comfort status, such as pain
  - comfort compared with environmental conditions (hot, cold, noisy, etc.)
  - the frequency of the occurrence of the behavior
  - the length of time of each occurrence
  - the severity of the occurrence (use measurable terms)
  - how the behavior affects the resident's function
  - the actions taken by staff to manage the behavior
  - the resident's response to staff intervention
  - healthcare provider and responsible party notifications
- Initiate
  - a social service/mental health referral and document your request
  - a behavior observation flow sheet
  - 24-hour monitoring
- Update care plan

Blood clots

The types of blood clots include the following:

- Embolus: a mass or clot of particles (may be gas or solid) that moves throughout the bloodstream.
- Phlebothrombosis: development of a clot within a vein without inflammation.
- Pulmonary embolus (PE): thrombus that forms above or in the popliteal vein that presents a high risk for migration to the pulmonary circulation.
- Thrombosis: a state in which a blood clot forms in a blood vessel.
- Thrombus: a stationary blood clot.
- Thrombophlebitis: inflammation of a vein accompanied by clot or thrombus formation; commonly occurs in veins deep in the lower extremities. Of the blood clots listed, this is the most common in long-term care. It is also called a deep vein thrombosis (DVT) because of its location.

Assess and document the following each shift:

- Vital signs
- Capillary refill
- Initiation of pulse oximetry
- Whether the resident has recently bumped or injured his or her legs
- Pedal pulse

- Femoral, popliteal, and posterior tibial pulse once every 24 hours, or as indicated
- Calf pain that increases on dorsiflexion of the foot (positive Homans' sign)
- Heat
- Redness
- Edema along the length of the affected vein
- Capillary refill less than two seconds
- Fever
- Malaise
- Fatigue
- Anorexia
- Pain
- Localized cyanosis; abnormal color
- Localized cool temperature
- Due to the nature of the condition, also monitor vital signs, presence or absence of chest pain, and shortness of breath

Cerebrovascular accident (CVA)

Signs of an impending CVA

Assess and document the following each shift:

- Severe headache
- Hypertension
- Numbness or weakness of one side of the body (face, an arm, or a leg)
- Mental confusion
- Difficulty speaking or understanding
- Impaired muscular coordination
- Impaired ability to walk

Immediately after a CVA

Assess and document the following each shift:

- Vital signs.
- Pulse oximetry.
- Capillary refill.
- Unconsciousness (initially).
- Level of consciousness, which can range from lethargy and confusion to coma that can persist for days or weeks. The length of the coma is an indication of prognosis. The longer the coma, the less likely that consciousness will return.

- Noisy, labored respirations.
- Confusion.
- Emotional lability.
- Whether eyes deviate toward the affected side of the brain.
- Whether cheek on the side of the CVA blows out on exhalation.
- Slow, full, bounding pulse.
- Hypertension.
- Temperature elevation (persists for several days).
- Hemiplegia on the side opposite the affected area of the brain.
- Hemiparesis (less common).
- Whether affected side of the body becomes flaccid immediately after CVA. This progresses to spasticity; the affected arm is usually more spastic than the leg.
- Expressive aphasia (inability to speak).
- Receptive aphasia (inability to understand spoken and written language).
- Hemianopsia on affected side (blindness in half the visual field of one or both eyes).

Chemotherapy

Assess and document the following each shift:

- Elevated temperature (may be masked by steroids or antiinflammatory drugs)
- Vital signs
- Lung sounds (describe)
- Bowel sounds (describe)
- Presence or absence of dyspnea at rest
- Dyspnea on exertion
- Presence of absence of cough:
  - If present, describe whether it's productive or nonproductive
  - If productive, describe appearance of sputum
- Complaints of anorexia
- Presence or absence of nausea/vomiting
- Presence or absence of sores in mouth
- Complaints of sore throat
- Presence or absence of urgency, dysuria, or any other change in voiding pattern
- Condition of skin, mucous membranes (note that the area between the gums and cheek will stay moist even with a mouth breather *unless resident is dehydrated*)

- Skin turgor (describe)
- Condition of skin (e.g., redness, swelling, drainage)
- Drainage from eyes or ears
- Hair loss
- Complaints of weakness or dizziness
- Presence or absence of perineal pain or discomfort
- Intake and output
- Psychological response to condition (describe)

Chest pain

Chest pain is a serious medical emergency. When a resident reports chest pain, do the following:

- Check the vital signs
- Check capillary refill
- Initiate pulse oximetry
- Notify the healthcare provider
- Provide oxygen at 3 liters/minute per cannula and increase according to degree of resident's distress, cyanosis, etc.
- Complete a quick physical assessment, including heart and lung sounds
- Check peripheral pulses bilaterally
- Check blood pressure in both arms
- Assess for trauma, edema, and bleeding

After these initial interventions, use the PQRST mnemonic to obtain additional information:

P—provoked or palliative:

- What caused or preceded the chest pain? What was the resident doing (activity) when the pain began?

Q—quality:

- Provide a description of the pain—for example, crushing, stabbing, like an elephant standing on the chest, etc. Use the resident's words in quotes.

R—region and radiation:

- Where did the pain begin? Does it radiate? If so, to where? It may be helpful to instruct the resident to point to a specific spot. Otherwise he or she may gesture to the entire chest.

S—severity of pain:

- Ask the resident to rate the pain on a scale of 1–10, with 1 being the least and 10 being the most painful.

T—time:

- Ask the resident to state at what time the pain began and describe the duration.

Note: Also see "Myocardial infarction."

Compartment syndrome

Definition

Compartment syndrome is a painful condition that occurs when pressure within the muscles builds up, preventing blood and oxygen from reaching muscles and nerves. This is a very serious complication that may develop following an injury or surgical procedure. It is common in long-bone fractures and musculoskeletal conditions in which there is no fracture. The most common location of compartment syndrome in adults is in a fractured tibia. The most common location of compartment syndrome in children is the humerus.

Compartment syndrome develops gradually over several hours. Bleeding or swelling occurs in the muscle tissue under the fascia. Occasionally, pressure from a cast or compression device also increases the pressure from the outside. If the swelling is not relieved, pressure on the muscles and nerves builds. Eventually, the pressure inside the fascia compartment will exceed the blood pressure, causing the capillaries to collapse. Blood flow to the muscles and nerves stops. If it is not restored promptly, tissue death begins.

Signs, symptoms, and documentation

- Severe pain, especially with movement or stretching (most common symptom)
- Pain seems out of proportion to the injury
- Tenderness with even gentle palpation
- Pain with deep breathing

- Tingling
- Burning
- Numbness
- Prickling
- Feeling of tightness or fullness in the affected muscle
- Abnormal sensations in the affected area (resident may not be able to describe them)
- Weakness in or inability to use the muscle
- The extremity may appear pale, cyanotic, or red.
- The skin of an extremity without a cast may feel warm to the touch, but the fingers and toes of a casted extremity feel cool to touch
- Edema
- Loss of the pulse in the extremity (a late, ominous sign)

Note: Compartment syndrome is a surgical emergency. The resident must be transferred to the acute care hospital quickly for care. Use a 911 ambulance.

Congestive heart failure (CHF)

Definitions

Heart failure is the inability of the heart to pump blood to the body parts sufficient to meet metabolic demands.

Types of heart failure include the following:

- **Acute heart failure:** sudden onset of the inability of the heart to contract; may cause life-threatening signs and symptoms, including pulmonary edema.
- **Chronic heart failure:** compromise in the ability of the heart to pump efficiently; often occurs as a result of another chronic disorder. When a resident has chronic heart failure, he or she develops signs and symptoms of both right-sided and left-sided heart failure.
- **CHF:** an accumulation of blood and fluid in tissues and organs from impaired circulation (figure 2.1).

Figure 2.1

This x-ray reveals congestive heart failure secondary to chronic hypertension. The enlarged cardiac silhouette is due to the effects of chronic high blood pressure on the left ventricle. The heart becomes enlarged, and fluid accumulates in the lungs.

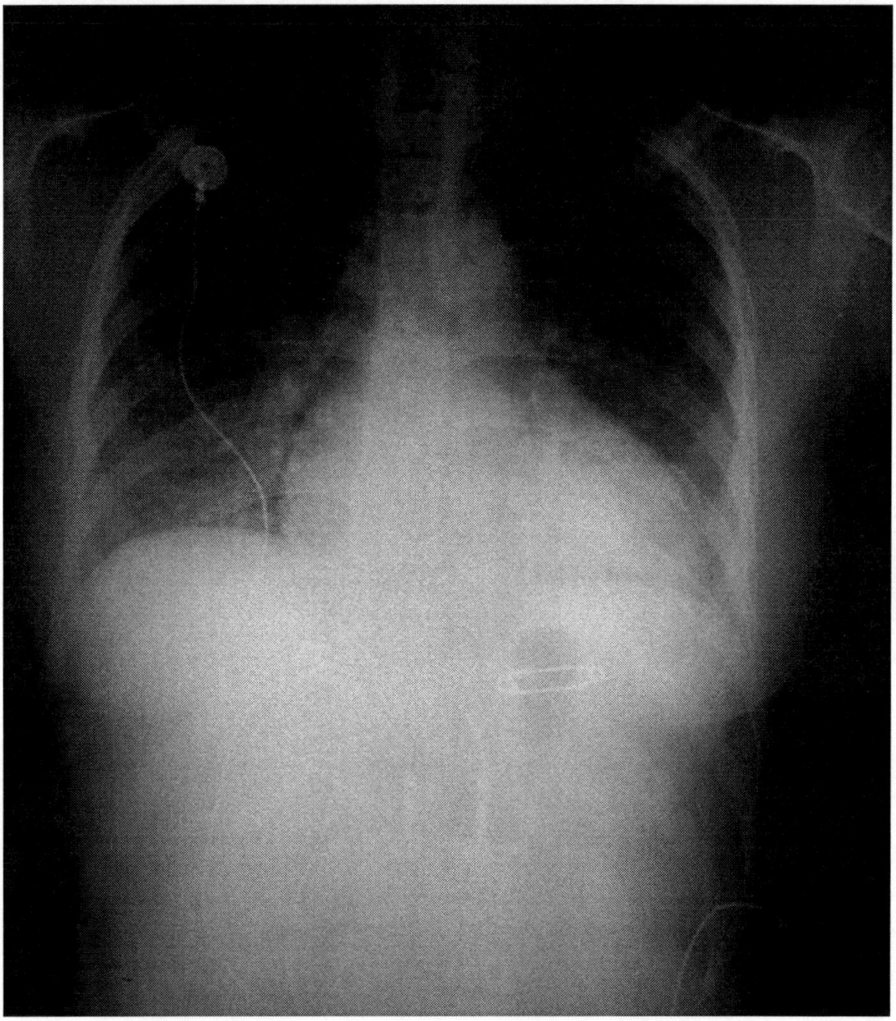

Courtesy of Centers for Disease Control and Prevention.

Assess and document the following each shift:

Right-sided heart failure

- Ascites
- Nausea/vomiting
- Weight gain
- Jugular venous distention
- Weakness
- Edema, fluid retention
- Gradual weight gain
- Rings, shoes, clothing seem tight as edema progresses
- Dependent pitting edema in feet and ankles
- Edema may disappear at night but recurs when awake
- Dysrhythmias
- Enlarged abdominal organs

Left-sided heart failure

- Unusual fatigue with minimal activity
- Exertional dyspnea
- Hypoxia
- Orthopnea
- Paroxysmal nocturnal dyspnea
- Fatigue
- Cyanosis
- Crackles
- Cough
- Expectorates pink, frothy sputum
- Rapid, irregular pulse
- Elevated blood pressure
- Decreased urine output
- Progressive restlessness and confusion
- Anorexia
- Nausea
- Flatulence

For both types of heart failure, assess and document the following:

- Vital signs.
- Capillary refill.
- Initiate pulse oximetry.
- Recent laboratory values, if any.
- New medications and side effects, if any.
- Signs/symptoms of dehydration or inadequate fluid intake (which causes hypovolemia). Consider I&O monitoring.
- Any other changes from resident's usual condition (i.e., what he or she is like on a normal day).
- Most recent PT and INR, coagulation status, and signs of internal bleeding if resident is on warfarin.

Note: Also see "Prerenal azotemia and acute renal failure."

Constipation, fecal impaction

Each shift, do the following and document the results:

- Evaluate abdomen by auscultation, percussion, and palpation.
- Determine the date of last bowel movement.
- Evaluate and document any of the following signs and symptoms:
    - Abdominal cramping
    - Bloating
    - Firm/distended abdomen
    - Straining during elimination
    - Small, hard, or dry feces
    - Distant or muffled bowel sounds
    - Backache
    - Headache
    - Reduced activity (inactivity, quieter than usual, sluggishness)
    - Low-grade fever (use oral or tympanic method, if possible)
    - Nausea and/or vomiting
    - Lethargy
    - Liquid stools
    - Pain, fullness, or discomfort in rectum

- Check for impaction.
- Monitor for signs/symptoms of dehydration or inadequate fluid intake (which causes hypovolemia).
- Consider I&O monitoring
- Increase fluid intake. Include in care plan the need to push fluids.
- Document/describe nursing actions and intervention:
  - Describe the resident's response to nursing intervention
  - Document healthcare provider and responsible party notifications
- Initiate 24-hour monitoring for abdominal assessment.

Death of resident

Early phase of dying

Assess and document the following each shift:

- Restlessness
- Confusion
- Agitation
- Wanting to reposition frequently
- Withdrawal from active participation in social activities
- Increased periods of sleep, lethargy
- Decreased intake of food and fluids
- Beginning to have periods of apnea whether awake or asleep
- Sees people who have already died
- States that he or she is dying
- Requests family be called to settle "unfinished business" and tie up "loose ends"
- Inability to heal or recover from wounds or infections
- Increased edema of either the extremities or the entire body (anasarca)

Signs and symptoms of impending death

Dying is unique to each person. Signs and symptoms will vary slightly. Assess and document the following:

- Sleeping more
- Loss of interest in food and fluids
- Nose, ears, hands, arms, feet, and legs may feel progressively cool to touch
- Skin, especially hands and feet, may appear cyanotic, mottled, and blotchy
- Skin may feel diaphoretic and clammy
- Rattling sounds in throat and lungs
- Loss of bowel and bladder control
- Restlessness
- Disorientation
- Breathing pattern changes to Cheyne-Stokes
- Blood pressure and pulse decrease
- Some people have a sudden burst of energy (becoming more alert and more talkative)
- Some people see persons or objects that are not visible to you

Pronouncement of death

This section applies only if permitted by state law and the written policies of your facility. An RN or a physician assistant may determine and pronounce a resident dead in situations other than when an individual is being supported by artificial means that preclude determination that the person's spontaneous respiratory and circulatory functions have ceased.

Assess and document the following:

- Respirations ceased, no spontaneous respirations
- No palpable pulses
- Unable to auscultate apical pulse
- Pupils fixed and dilated; eyes may be open slightly
- Jaw relaxed; may be open slightly
- Skin cool to touch
- Skin mottled (e.g., gray, cyanotic, lividity, etc.)
- Algor mortis (i.e., reduction in body temperature following death)
- Rigor mortis, if present
- Postmortem care given
- Disposition of medications and personal belongings
- Notification of healthcare provider, next of kin, coroner, or justice of the peace, according to local regulation
- Order to release the body

Dehydration, actual or risk for

Dehydration is the most common fluid and electrolyte disorder seen in elderly persons. It occurs when loss of body fluid (water) exceeds fluid intake, which is why I&O measurement and assessment are of key importance in this population. Dehydration is associated with a high mortality rate. However, it continues to be inadequately prevented, underrecognized, unreported (to the healthcare provider), and untreated. Dehydration is likely if the resident has decreased intake as well as two or more of the signs and symptoms listed here. Assess residents carefully and maintain a high level of suspicion.

Do the following to assess and document dehydration:

- Check for and consider recent laboratory values, if any.
- Evaluate new medications and side effects, if any.
- Monitor for signs/symptoms of dehydration, inadequate fluid intake (which causes hypovolemia).
- Consider I&O monitoring
- Note any other changes from the resident's usual condition (i.e., what he or she is like on a normal day).

Assess and document the following each shift:

- Vital signs
- Capillary refill
- Sunken cheeks

- Sunken eyeballs
- Dry, brown tongue and mucous membranes (note that the area between the gums and cheek will stay moist even with a mouth breather *unless resident is dehydrated*)
- Furrows or lines in tongue
- Dry, inelastic skin
- Poor skin turgor (forehead or over the sternum)
- Weight loss, usually more than 3 lb. weight loss within seven days
- Postural hypotension
- Dizziness, lightheadedness
- Falls
- Hypotension
- Tachycardia
- Elevated temperature
- Weakness, particularly in the upper body
- Mental confusion
- Decreased output, oliguria
- Concentrated urine
- Constipation and fecal impaction
- Nausea and anorexia
- Increased time for veins to refill

- Delusions, dizziness, delirium
- Unsteady gait
- Headache
- Flushed appearance
- Presence/absence of diaphoresis
- Presence of any medical conditions or orders that predispose resident to dehydration (e.g., fluid restriction order, diabetes diagnosis)
- Medication regimen—determine whether diuretics are being given or if the medication regimen accounts for fluid loss (e.g., laxatives causing liquid stools)
- Abnormal laboratory values (e.g., elevated hemoglobin/hematocrit, potassium, chloride, sodium, creatinine, BUN/creatinine ratio, albumin, transferrin, BUN, urine specific gravity)
- Essential laboratory values:
  - BUN over 22 mg/dl
  - Elevated hematocrit (greater than three times the hemoglobin)
  - Potassium below 3.5
  - Chloride over 107
  - Sodium over 147 suggests severe dehydration
  - Elevated serum creatinine
  - A creatinine greater than 1.5 suggests renal disease—if greater than 1.5, determine the BUN/creatinine ratio by dividing the BUN by the creatinine; values over 23 suggest dehydration

Evaluation/approximation of dehydration

Approximate degree of dehydration	Signs and symptoms
0–1%	Thirst
2%–5%	Dry mouth, flushed skin, fatigue, headache, impaired physical performance
6%	Increased body temperature, pulse, and respirations; dizziness; increased weakness
8%	Dizziness, increased weakness, labored breathing with exercise
10%	Muscle spasms, swollen tongue, delirium
11%	Poor blood circulation, failing kidney function

Note: Also see "Prerenal azotemia and acute renal failure"

Diabetic residents, observations of

Do the following during each shift:

- Check for and consider recent laboratory values, if any.
- Evaluate new medications and side effects, if any.
- Monitor for signs/symptoms of dehydration or inadequate fluid intake (which causes hypovolemia). Consider I&O monitoring.
- Note any other changes from the resident's usual condition (i.e., what he or she is like on a normal day)

Assess and document the following each shift:

- Inadequate food intake
- Eating food not allowed on diet
- Refusal of meals, supplements, or snacks
- Nausea, vomiting, or diarrhea
- Inadequate fluid intake
- Excessive activity
- Complaints of dizziness, shakiness, or racing heart
- Blood sugar values outside of normal range

Diabetes, unstable or potential for instability

- Check for and consider recent laboratory values, if any.
- Evaluate new medications and side effects, if any.
- Monitor for signs/symptoms of dehydration or inadequate fluid intake (which causes hypovolemia). Consider I&O monitoring.
- Note any other changes from the resident's usual condition (i.e., what he or she is like on a normal day).

Document that you perform the following each shift:

- Check vital signs.
- Take fingerstick blood sugar, as often as necessary, based on food intake and insulin.
- Provide diet and medications appropriate to treat the resident's medical condition.
- Assess the resident's dietary intake pattern and nutritional status.
- Monitor and accurately record the resident's food consumption. Offer substitutes for uneaten foods.
- Monitor the resident's weight monthly or more often, if indicated, and report changes to the healthcare provider.
- Observe the resident during each shift for signs and symptoms of diabetic-related complications.
- Check for signs/symptoms of hyperglycemia:
  - Nausea, vomiting

- Weakness
- Headache
- Full, bounding pulse
- Fruity smell to breath
- Hot, dry, flushed skin
- Labored respirations
- Drowsiness
- Mental confusion
- Unconsciousness
- Sugar in the urine
- High blood sugar by fingerstick

• Check for signs/symptoms of hypoglycemia:

- Complaints of hunger, weakness, dizziness, or shakiness
- Skin cold, moist, clammy, pale
- Rapid, shallow respirations
- Nervousness and excitement
- Rapid pulse
- Unconsciousness
- No sugar in the urine
- Low blood sugar by fingerstick

- Provide adequate fluid intake:
  - Monitor and document I&O until established that intake is sufficient
  - Write a narrative evaluation regarding I&O sufficiency and fluid balance each shift
- Monitor and document the resident's blood sugar routinely—four times daily or more often—until a stable pattern is established. Thereafter, monitor the resident's blood sugar daily to weekly, depending on stability.
- Monitor and document the resident's blood sugar immediately at any time that the resident shows signs or symptoms of diabetic crisis (i.e., decreasing level of consciousness; signs or symptoms of infection; increasing confusion or disorientation; rapid, shallow respiration; rapid, weak pulse; warm to hot, dry, flushed skin; increased thirst; decreased skin turgor).
- Recognize that signs and symptoms of infection can cause rapid changes in the resident's blood sugar. Provide extra monitoring for signs and symptoms of diabetic crisis if signs or symptoms of infection are present.
- Immediately report abnormalities in blood sugar to the healthcare provider and give emergency treatment as indicated or ordered. Recheck blood sugar if insulin is ordered and administered to determine whether the intervention was effective. Continue ongoing monitoring.
- If the healthcare provider is not immediately available or does not respond, contact the alternate healthcare provider listed on the resident's medical record. If this healthcare provider is not immediately available, contact the facility medical director. If none of these healthcare providers is immediately available, or if the resident's condition is emergent, send the resident to the emergency department via 911 emergency ambulance.

- Routinely monitor for and record observations and changes in the resident's condition and services provided in the clinical record.
- Document/describe nursing actions and intervention:
  - Describe the resident's response to nursing intervention
  - Document notifications to the healthcare provider and responsible party, when indicated
- Update care plan for increased monitoring and schedule to address change in condition during next care conference.
- Initiate 24-hour monitoring and continue monitoring for at least 24 hours after condition has fully stabilized.

Discharge

- If discharging home or to another facility, document evidence of resident/responsible party teaching:
  - Complete and send a recapitulation of resident stay/discharge summary with the resident. Keep a copy with the chart.
- Photocopy the resident's comprehensive assessment and other appropriate documents, such as the history and physical, healthcare provider orders, and medication records if transferring to the hospital or another long-term care facility.
- Prepare a standard resident transfer form if transferring to the hospital or another long-term care facility:
  - At the time of discharge, give copies of the documents listed above to the ambulance personnel or responsible party for transfer to the receiving facility
- Conduct a care conference with the resident or responsible party in which the resident's overall plan of care is described. Develop a post-discharge plan of care listing problems, goals, and approaches to use to provide continuity of care:
  - Photocopy the post-discharge plan of care and retain a copy for the resident's medical record
- Obtain a telephone order or other healthcare provider order authorizing discharge.

- Pack the resident's belongings and check them against the personal inventory sheet, if discharging home or to another long-term care facility. Ask the resident or responsible party to sign the inventory.
- Dress the resident appropriately for transfer. Consider the season, weather conditions, and method of transportation.
- Provide instructions to the individual who will be accompanying the resident for care during transfer, if necessary.
- Provide medications and supplies needed during the transfer and instruct the individual accompanying the resident in their use, if appropriate.
- Document
  - event(s), if any, leading to discharge
  - full resident assessment, including skin assessment
  - complete vital signs
  - overview of general condition
  - to where, with whom, and by what method of transportation the resident was discharged
  - disposition of medications
  - disposition of personal belongings
- Remove all open chart forms, such as MAR and ADL flow sheets, from active records. File with the chart. Check the narcotics book. Remove sign-out sheets for control drugs. Continue to keep narcotics locked and counted each shift until they are discarded or picked up, according to facility policy.

Dysphagia

Dysphagia is difficulty swallowing food, fluids, or oral secretions. Approximately 53%–74% of long-term care facility residents have dysphagia. Most people swallow at least 600 times each day. People with dysphagia may swallow two or three times more than this, making swallowing an insurmountable problem. Residents with dysphagia are at great risk for weight loss, malnutrition, dehydration, choking, aspiration, and aspiration pneumonia. Residents who are at high risk for developing dysphagia include those who

- have a neuromuscular diseases (Parkinson's disease, Huntington's chorea, or multiple sclerosis)
- have had a stroke
- have cancer of the head, neck, or esophagus
- have had radiation treatment to the face or throat
- are on medications that decrease saliva production, impair cognition, or increase sedation
- have dementia

Signs and symptoms

Assess and document the following each shift:

- Difficulty controlling liquids and secretions in the mouth
- Having a wet- or gurgly sounding voice

- Taking a long time to begin a swallow
- Needing to swallow three to four times for each bite of food
- Having a feeling of fullness or tightness in the throat or chest
- Having a sensation of food sticking in the esophagus or sternal area
- Coughing/choking
- Frequent throat clearing
- Lack of a gag reflex
- Weak cough before, during, or after a swallow
- Pocketing food
- Spitting food out
- Refusing to eat
- Recurrent upper respiratory infections
- Persistent low-grade fever
- Unintentional weight loss

Edema

Assess and document the following each shift:

- Check weight daily. Monitor for trends, gains, losses.
- Check vital signs.
- Check capillary refill.
- Initiate pulse oximetry, if shortness of breath is present.
- Strictly monitor intake and output:
  - If incontinent, weigh briefs (1 g weight = approximately 1 mL fluid)
- Note fluid restriction and resident compliance, if ordered.
- Note appearance of fluid in face, fingers, abdomen, legs, or feet.
- Assess lung sounds; lungs clear.
- Insert urinary catheter, if appropriate.
- Monitor hydration status (e.g., appearance of mucous membranes, adequacy of pulses, orthostatic blood pressure—note that the area between the gums and cheek will stay moist even with a mouth breather *unless resident is dehydrated*).
- Monitor labs related to fluid retention, such as urine specific gravity, sodium, BUN, creatinine, decreased hematocrit, increased urine osmolality.
- Monitor urine specific gravity in facility; generally speaking, the normal value of a random urine specimen is between 1.015 and 1.025. After 12

hours without fluid intake, urinary-specific gravity is approximately 1.022. After 24 hours without fluids, specific gravity is 1.026. Urine becomes more concentrated and odor becomes stronger as specific gravity increases. Specific gravity of 1.035 suggests renal failure or severe dehydration.

- Note that sudden onset of significant facial edema with or without respiratory distress suggests an allergy and impending anaphylaxis. Notify the healthcare provider promptly.

Identifying and monitoring edema

Nursing personnel should monitor edema and inform the healthcare provider of the presence of this condition, as well as changes in the amount of fluid retained. Types of edema include the following:

- **Nonpitting edema:** may be localized to one area, or generalized throughout the body (anasarca). The skin appears shiny and taut.
- **Periorbital edema:** occurs around the orbits of the eyes.
- **Peripheral edema:** occurs in the hands, lower legs, and feet.
- **Pitting edema:** occurs when there is obvious fluid in the skin. It retains an indentation caused by palpation of the skin.

Evaluating edema

Nursing personnel must use consistent means of evaluating and documenting pitting edema. Measure over the tibia, behind the medial malleolus, and over the dorsum of each foot. Press your index finger over the bony prominence for several seconds. Any depression that does not rebound rapidly and resume its original contour almost immediately is a sign of pitting edema (figure 2.2). This may also be called **orthostatic edema**.

When assessing the resident, note and document:

- No edema present
- Nonpitting edema present
- Pitting edema present (quantify using edema scale)

Figure 2.2

The feet reveal pitting edema, which occurs as a result of pressure applied by an examiner's fingertips upon the skin, causing an indentation in the swollen, fluid-filled tissue that persists for a long period of time after the release of the pressure.

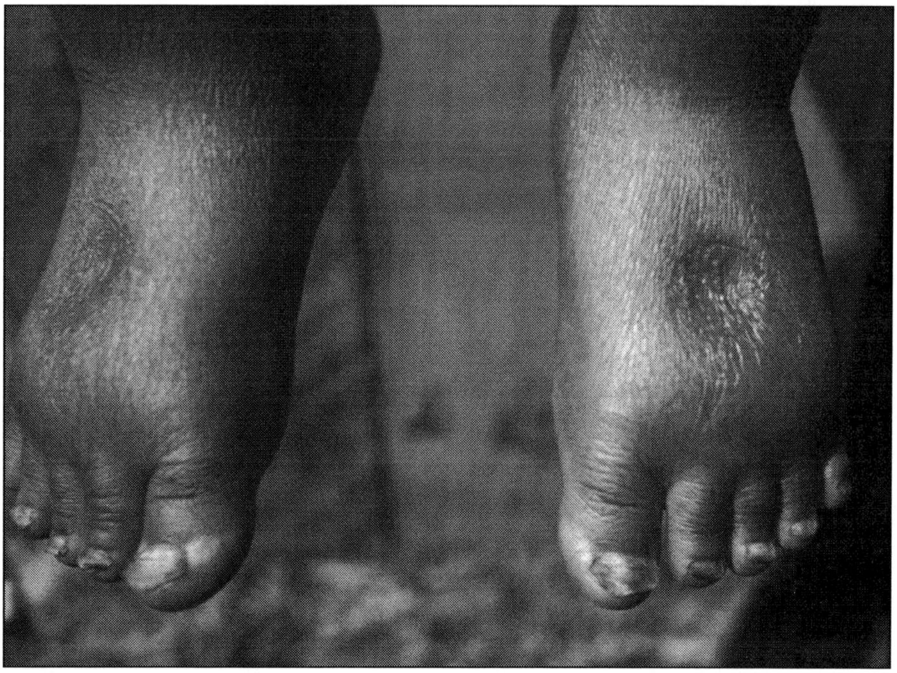

Courtesy of Centers for Disease Control and Prevention.

Quantifying pitting edema #1

+1 = slight pitting (about 2 mm depression), no visible distortion, disappears rapidly

+2 = greater depth (approximately 4 mm), no visible distortion of extremity, disappears in 10–15 seconds

+3 = visible change in limb contour, definite pit (approximately 6 mm), persists for more than one minute

+4 = grossly distorted limb, very deep pit (approximately 8 mm) lasting 2–5 minutes

Quantifying pitting edema #2

1+ = 2 mm indentation, barely detectable

2+ = 4 mm indentation (3 mm–5mm indentation)

3+ = 6 mm indentation (5 mm–10 mm indentation)

4+ = 8 mm indentation (more than 8 mm indentation; some authorities say more than 10 mm)

Note: Also see "Prerenal azotemia and acute renal failure."

Falls

Falls include sliding out of a chair and lowering a resident to the floor. Immediately notify a healthcare provider if sutures are needed or if you suspect a:

- fracture
- head injury
- neck injury

The first priority is to stabilize the resident and make sure he or she receives proper emergency care. You will make notifications, document the incident, and complete reports.

Review the following and report to the healthcare provider, as appropriate:

- Describe unusual signs/symptoms *prior to fall*, if any, such as
    - increased confusion
    - weakness, dizziness, or lightheadedness
    - chest pain
    - dyspnea
    - slurred speech
    - gait change
    - other potential contributing conditions

- Describe unusual *post-fall* signs and/or symptoms, if any, such as
  - weakness, dizziness, lightheadedness
  - pain
  - dyspnea
  - slurred speech
  - seizure activity
  - inability to move
  - loss of consciousness or change in level of consciousness/mental status
- Note new medications, adverse reactions, and side effects, if any.
- Monitor for signs/symptoms of dehydration and inadequate fluid intake (which causes hypovolemia). Consider I&O monitoring.
- Note any other changes from resident's usual condition (i.e., what he or she is like on a normal day).
- If the resident is on warfarin, review and report most recent PT and INR, coagulation status, and signs of internal bleeding.
- Check for and consider other recent laboratory values, if any.

Next, establish a monitoring system for the following:

- Vital signs
- Neurological checks
- Evaluation using Glasgow Coma Scale and ABCD Stroke Scale
- Notifications

- Implementation of neurological checks and head injury monitoring if the fall was not witnessed (initial documentation should note whether the incident was witnessed):
    - Document the anatomic position in which the resident was found
- Recognition that the resident's fall risk has just increased; update the care plan
- Assessing and evaluating causative and contributing factors
- Evaluating social behavior (whether confusion, denial of ability, or other comparable factors contributed to fall)
- Determining the reason why a resident was found on the floor after an unknown period of time, if applicable
- Determining whether unmet needs contributed to the fall
- **Evaluating the orthostatic blood pressure**[1] (this is an important, and often omitted, step)
- Reviewing and evaluating the medication regimen (research has shown that fall risk increases when residents take four or more medications[2]):
    - Be suspicious if resident is on a new medication; inform the healthcare provider
- Assessing the resident for signs and symptoms of acute illness and determining where he or she is regarding length of stay (almost 25% of falls are related to an acute illness,[3] and many falls occur during the first few days of admission, when the individual is unfamiliar with the environment)
- Determining whether loss of sensation (feeling) contributed to the fall (loss of feeling occurs because of many medical conditions; we collect position and balance information from our legs and feet, and, to a lesser extent, the hands;

thus residents with peripheral neuropathy, stroke, diabetes, and other conditions have lost these sensations, so it stands to reason that impaired sensation and complete sensory loss affect fall risk)

- Determining whether uncorrected vision or hearing problems contributed to the fall
- Consider whether pain was a fall risk factor for the resident (residents who are in pain tend to be less active and may assume peculiar positions when ambulating and transferring to compensate for the pain—for example, their movements may be stilted or rigid)

1. *Orthostatic hypotension* is the most common cardiovascular risk factor for falls, and the risk increases in persons over age 70. This problem involves a transient systolic blood pressure reduction of at least 20 mmHg when the resident assumes an upright position. Volume depletion, bleeding, diarrhea, and certain medications commonly cause orthostasis, although many other factors may induce the problem. The drop in blood pressure reduces blood flow to the brain, precipitating dizziness, loss of balance, or fainting that results in a fall. (Colgan, J. 2001. Syncope: a fall from grace. *Prog Cardiovasc Nurs.* 2001, 17(2):66–71.)
2. A toolkit of best practices for care of the elderly. 2001. *Presentation. Ontario Hospital Association Conference.* Online. *www.joannabriggs.edu.au*. Accessed 12/22/02.
3. Kuehm, AF, and Sendelweck, S. 1995. Acute health status and its relationship to falls in the nursing home. *J Gerontol Nurs.* 1995, 21(7):41–49.

Fractures

Definitions

Fractures are classified by the type of break in the bone and whether the skin is broken:

- A **complete fracture** is a break across the entire cross section of the bone. It is often **displaced**, or improperly aligned, and must be reduced and straightened.
- An **incomplete fracture** involves only part of the cross section of bone.
- A **closed or simple fracture** occurs when the skin is intact and not broken.
- An **open or compound fracture** (figure 2.3), occurs when the skin over the fracture is broken. The bone may or may not protrude.
- A **pathologic fracture** is a fracture in a diseased bone. It occurs as a result of osteoporosis, a tumor, or cancer.
- A **hip fracture** is a fracture of the upper third of the femur or head of the femur. The term describes a break of the proximal femur at the connection, where it angles into the hip socket.

Figure 2.3

This open fracture protruded through the skin then retracted, leaving an obvious injury.

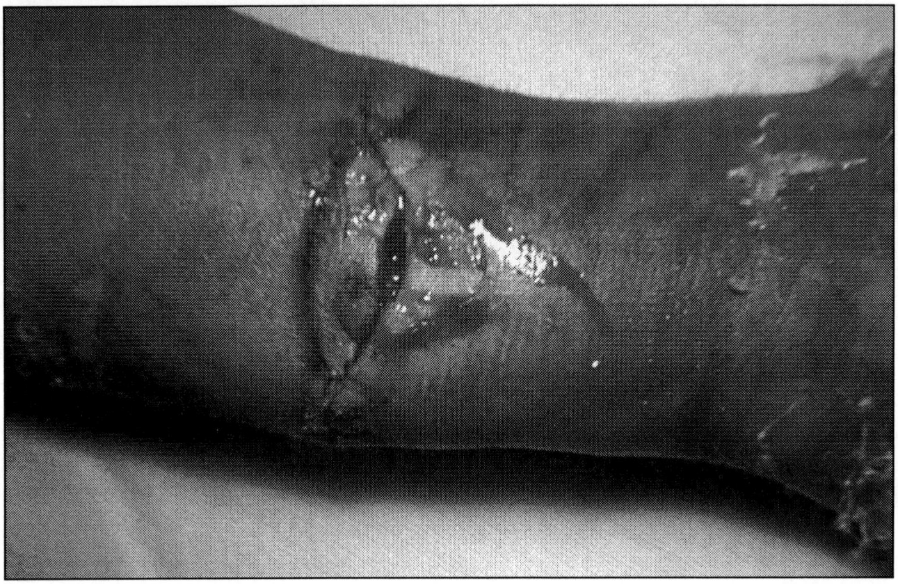

Courtesy of Centers for Disease Control and Prevention.

The pattern of a fracture describes the manner in which the bone is broken:

- A **greenstick fracture** occurs when one side of the bone is broken and the other side is bent. It is most common in children, whose bone growth is incomplete. The bones tend to bend like young trees, hence the name "greenstick fracture."
- A **transverse fracture** breaks completely across the bone.
- An **oblique fracture** is a fracture that runs at an angle across the bone.
- A **spiral fracture** twists around the bone.

- A **comminuted fracture** involves shattering and splintering of the bone into three or more fragments.
- A **depressed fracture** is seen only in fractures of the skull and bones of the face. This type of fracture depresses the bone and drives fragments inward.
- A **compression fracture** is seen only in the vertebrae of the spine. This type of fracture collapses the bone inward.
- An **avulsion fracture** occurs when a bone fragment is pulled off at the point of ligament or tendon attachment.
- An **impacted fracture** occurs when the fragment from one bone is wedged into another bone.
- An **epiphyseal fracture** is a fracture through the epiphysis and is not seen in the geriatric population.

Hip fractures

The incidence of hip fractures increases with age, doubling for each decade beyond age 50.[1] In the United States, one of every three adults (living in any setting) over age 65 falls each year. More than 50% of all nursing facility residents fall each year. Of these, approximately 40% experience repeated falls. Of these, approximately 11% experience significant injuries associated with the fall.[2] Common injuries include hip fracture, which significantly increases mortality.

Falls are the leading cause of injury-related deaths in the elderly. Of all fractures from falls, hip fractures cause the greatest number of deaths and lead to the most severe health problems. Approximately 350,000 individuals are hospitalized for hip fracture annually in the United States. By the year 2050, there will be an estimated 650,000 hip fractures annually—and nearly 1,800 hip fractures a day. Ninety percent of these are the result of falls.[3] Hip fracture is a devastating injury for people of all ages—particularly the elderly. Only one in four patients recovers completely; 40% will require nursing facility care; 50% will need a cane or walker; and 24% of those over age 50 will die of complications within 12 months.[4]

Knowing the type of hip fracture is important because it determines the treatment and operative repair, postoperative care, and rehabilitation. The following are types of hip fractures:

- **Hip fracture:** the most common type of fracture in the elderly. The term "hip fracture" is a misnomer. This term refers to a fracture anywhere in the upper third or head of the femur. A hip fracture is a break of the proximal femur at the connection, where it angles into the hip socket.
- **Femoral neck fracture:** (45% of hip fractures) an intracapsular fracture one to two inches from the joint; proximal to greater and lesser trochanter; predisposes the resident to avascular necrosis if displaced.
- **Intertrochanteric fracture:** (45% of hip fractures) three to four inches from the joint; extracapsular; this is a very vascular area.
- **Subtrochanteric fracture:** (10% of hip fractures) between the distal and lesser trochanter.
- **Stress fracture:** a spontaneous, uncommon femur fracture as a result of severe osteoporosis. The resident may hear a pop in the bone. He or she may or may not fall. Signs and symptoms of a stress fracture may be subtle, such as pain in the groin or thigh. The pain increases with activity and may persist for hours afterward. It will eventually become constant, even without activity. This pain is generally in the groin; however, it can also be referred to the knee.

Assessment and documentation

Signs, symptoms, assessment, and documentation of fractures will vary with the type of fracture and location. Fractures are very painful. Movement is limited, if the resident can move at all. Some parts of the body, such as the area over the femur, are vascular and bleed readily under the skin. An ecchymosis the size of an adult's fist over the femur indicates the loss of approximately one pint of blood. Other common signs and symptoms to assess and document include the following:

- Resident is typically found on the floor, unable to get up or move the injured leg.
- Inability to stand or use the leg normally; occasionally, a resident with a fracture will be able to walk with difficulty, but most are unable to ambulate after a fall and hip fracture. A resident with a stress fracture may be able to walk with a limp.
- Pain may worsen upon pressure (palpation) or movement:
  - Pain is usually in the hip, but occasionally a resident may complain of knee pain
  - Assess pain using regular facility pain scales or tools
- Heel percussion and deep palpation in the inguinal area will cause pain.
- Pain or tenderness with palpation over the femoral neck.
- Loss of function—function depends on intact bone.
- Deformity—the extremity may be bent backward or in an unusual position. For example, a hip fracture often results in shortening and external rotation, with toes of the affected leg pointing outward. This is largely due to spasm in the strong muscles in the hip and femur area.

- Limited range of motion, particularly internal rotation—attempting range of motion may cause extreme pain; if so, stop the procedure.
- Unnatural or false motion at the site of the fracture.
- Crepitus—a grating sound of bone ends moving over one another may be audible.
- Edema—usually greatest directly over the fracture.
- Ecchymosis, skin injury—occurs when sharp bone fragments tear through soft tissue.
- Edema and ecchymosis may extend to the thigh, groin, or lower pelvic area.
- Spasm—the muscles in this area are among the largest and strongest in the body; muscles contract when the bone is fractured, and the spasticity contributes to the severe pain and shortening of the extremity.
- Paralysis—an infrequent complication, resulting from nerve damage.
- Numbness, tingling, or prickling—suggest nerve compression/damage, compartment syndrome, or both; instruct the resident to move fingers, toes, and unaffected extremities to increase circulation and indicate neurologic and motor function.
- Pulse—presense or absence of pulse distal to injury. (If absent, send to ER in 911 ambulance).

1. Ellis, TJ. 2003. Hip fractures in the elderly. *Current Women's Health Reports* 2003, 3:75–80.
2. Braun, J., and Capezuti, E. 2000. The legal and medical aspects of physical restraints and bed siderails and their relationship to falls and fall-related injuries in nursing homes. *DePaul Journal of Health Care Law* 2000, 4(1), 1–72.
3. AAOS Fact Sheet. *Falls and hip fractures*. Online. *orthoinfo.aaos.org/fact/thr_report.cfm?Thread_ID=77&topcategory=Hip*. Accessed 7/08/02.
4. AAOS Fact Sheet. *Hip fracture*. Online. *orthoinfo.aaos.org/fact/thr_report.cfm?Thread_ID=229&topcategory=Hip*. Accessed 7/08/02.

Gastrointestinal upset, distress, other related conditions

- Check for and consider recent laboratory values, if any.
- Evaluate new medications and side effects, if any.
- Monitor for signs/symptoms of dehydration or inadequate fluid intake (which causes hypovolemia). Consider I&O monitoring.
- Note any other changes from resident's usual condition (i.e., what he or she is like on a normal day).
- If resident is on warfarin, review and report most recent PT and INR, coagulation status, and signs of internal bleeding.
- Determine whether other residents in the facility are being treated for or have recently experienced the same or similar signs and symptoms.
- Determine/study whether a relationship exists between other factors and the signs or symptoms the resident currently exhibits. For example, if the resident complains of nausea and has had vomiting or diarrhea, is there a relationship between the vomiting and medication administration time, initial doses of new medication, time of day, intake of certain foods or fluids, etc.?

Assess and document the following each shift:

- Vital signs
- Presence of tachycardia
- Bowel sounds (describe)

- Inspection (auscultation, above), palpation, and percussion of abdomen
- Complaints of pain on palpation
- Presence or absence of nausea, vomiting, or diarrhea
- Presence of constipation or fecal impaction
- Adequacy of fluid intake
- Stools (describe)
- Presence of abdominal distention; if present, measure abdominal girth with tape measure
- Presence of abdominal rigidity
- Weight loss
- Complaints or signs/symptoms of dysphagia
- Complaints of reflux, heartburn
- Skin color; presence of jaundice
- Skin turgor (describe)
- Skin moisture and temperature (describe)
- Signs or symptoms of gastrointestinal bleeding
- Assess for symptoms of anemia, dehydration, malnutrition, weakness, or electrolyte imbalance
- Pain

Head injury, suspected head injury, or unwitnessed fall

Take and document the following actions each shift:

- Assess the resident for changes in level of consciousness, which is a cardinal sign of untoward pathology:
  - Assess the resident immediately after the fall, then frequently throughout the shift
  - Continue assessment for a minimum of 72 hours
- Check for obvious injuries to the scalp, including lacerations, bruises, or contusions
- Check vital signs
- Monitor and assess for confusion, memory loss, difficulty speaking, gait or balance problems, pupils of unequal size or reaction, headache, vomiting, visual disturbances, or periods of coherence alternating with periods of confusion or lethargy:
  - Continue monitoring for a minimum of 72 hours
- Perform frequent neurologic assessments, initially every 15 minutes, progressing to every 30 minutes, every 60 minutes, every four hours, to every eight hours after 24 hours:
  - Assessment should include, at a minimum, pulse, respiration, and blood pressure measurements; assessment of pupil size and reactivity; and equality of hand grasps

- Complete the Glasgow Coma Scale immediately, then once each shift
- Keep the resident's head elevated to reduce intracranial pressure
- Minimize resident movement
- Keep the environment subdued and the resident calm and stress free
- After the initial assessment, notify the healthcare provider and document his or her response and new orders:
  - Prepare the resident for an x-ray, CT scan, or other diagnostic tests, as ordered
- Notify the responsible party about the fall
- Administer analgesic medications, as ordered
- Update the care plan to reflect special monitoring related to the head injury:
  - After the acute phase has passed, reassess the cause of the resident's fall and take measures to prevent recurrence; describe these measures on the care plan
- Document all monitoring and the resident's response, even if findings are negative (no loss of consciousness, denies pain, etc.)
- Document/describe nursing actions and intervention:
  - Describe the resident's response to nursing intervention
- Initiate 72-hour monitoring

Head injury/potential subdural hematoma

Assess and document the following each shift. Use head injury, suspected head injury, or unwitnessed fall guidelines detailed in the previous section.

Onset of signs and symptoms may be insidious. Suspect a subdural hematoma if the resident shows

- confusion, memory loss
- weakness in one or more extremities
- ataxia, gait, or balance disturbances
- difficulty speaking, aphasia
- a visible injury, such as an old bruise or scab over the site of a previous head injury
- unequal pupil size or reaction
- vision deterioration (in acute subdural hematoma)
- an intense headache in acute subdural hematoma
- a recurrent, chronic headache in subacute and chronic hematomas
- changes in level of consciousness:
  - may be rapid in acute subdural hematoma
  - decline in level of consciousness slower in subacute subdural hematoma
  - in chronic subdural hematoma, the resident may alternate between periods of alertness, lethargy, and confusion

Definitions

The following are types of subdural hematoma:

- **Acute subdural hematoma:** the *onset of symptoms is rapid.* Mortality is approximately 50%. Survivors often have neurologic deficits.
- **Subacute subdural hematoma:** the onset of symptoms is gradual, with progressive neurologic decline occurring *over 24–36 hours.*
- **Chronic subdural hematoma:** produces neurologic signs and symptoms *up to six weeks after the initial injury*. Because of the prolonged period between the initial injury and manifestation of signs and symptoms, the resident and caregivers usually forget about the causative injury. They may not associate the current problem with a head injury from the recent past. This lesion can grow quite large before becoming symptomatic. The mortality rate for a chronic subdural hematoma is approximately 10% in the elderly.

Herpes zoster

Assess and document the following each shift:

- Severe pain, usually on one side of the body; pain may be present before lesions erupt
- Resident may describe the pain as burning, tearing, twisting, gnawing, or stabbing
- Rash erupts within 48–72 hours
- Rash progresses to tense, raised, fluid-filled vesicles in three to five days (figure 2.4); vesicles erupt along dermatomes supplied by cranial or spinal nerves
- Blisters often appear in groups that look similar to chickenpox and may be on one side of the body only; the base of the pustules is red and shiny:
    - *Note:* If blisters appear on the nose or near the eyes (figure 2.5), refer the resident to an ophthalmologist because complications in this area can be severe
- Resident may complain of itching
- Headache
- Low-grade fever
- Malaise
- Signs and symptoms of secondary bacterial infection of the lesions

Figure 2.4

The shingles pathogen may lay dormant in the spinal nerve roots through a chickenpox-infected individual's life, only manifesting its presence through outbreaks as shingles, or herpes zoster. It is caused by the *Herpesviridae chickenpoxvirus*. This pustulovesicular rash represents a new onset shingles outbreak due to the varicella-zoster virus (VZV) pathogen.

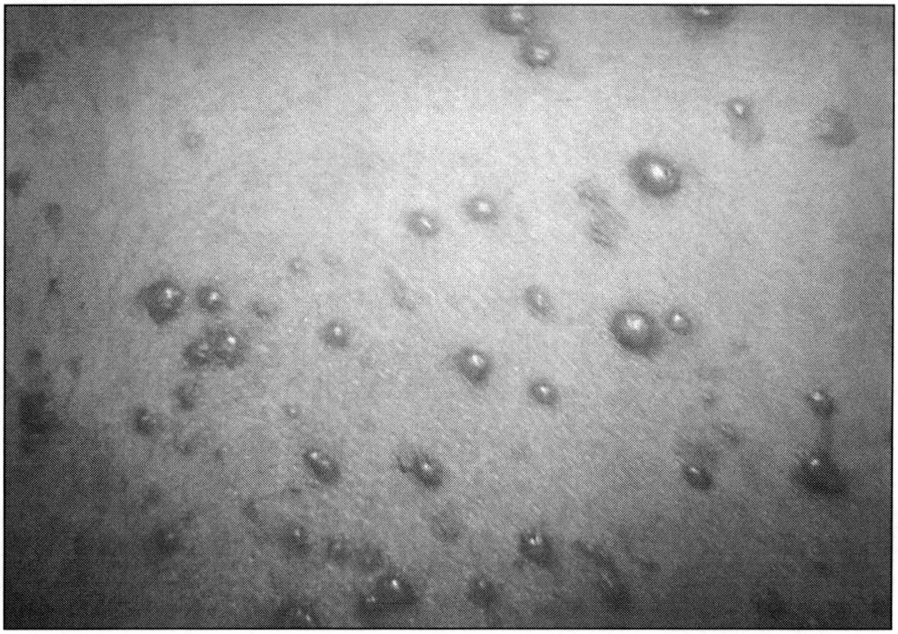

Courtesy of Centers for Disease Control and Prevention.

Figure 2.5

Ocular herpes is potentially a very serious condition needing prompt medical treatment.

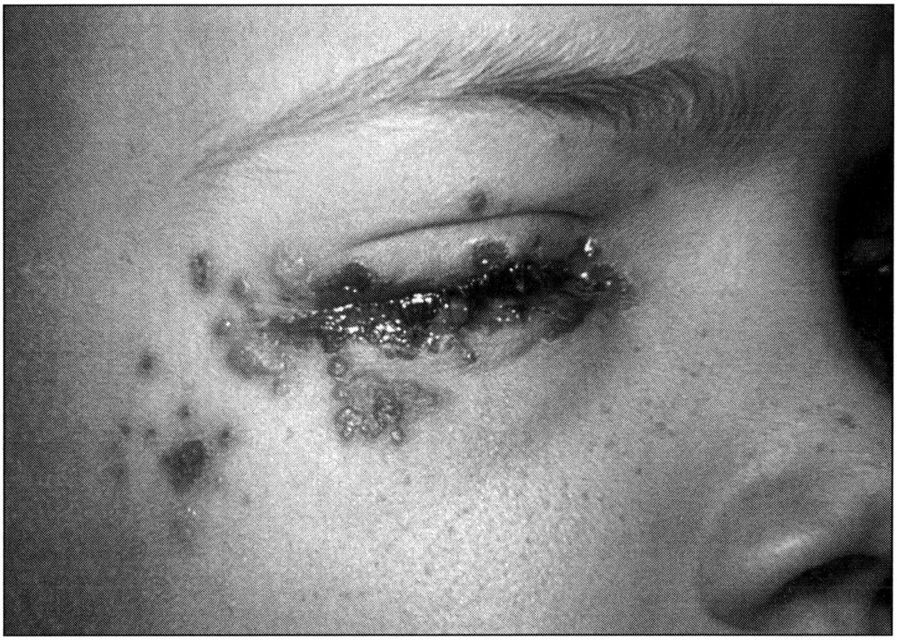

Courtesy of Centers for Disease Control and Prevention.

- Nursing comfort measures provided (e.g., cool compresses, calamine lotion, or domeboro soaks)
- As the condition progresses, the lesions burst, scab over, and begin to heal (figure 2.6)
- Presence or absence of postherpetic neuralgia (a condition in which constant, severe pain or periods of intermittent pain continue after the skin heals; it can last for years, and is more common in residents over age 70)

Figure 2.6

Shingles are no longer contagious when all the lesions have burst and are crusted over. However, the resident continues to experience pain and itching at this stage.

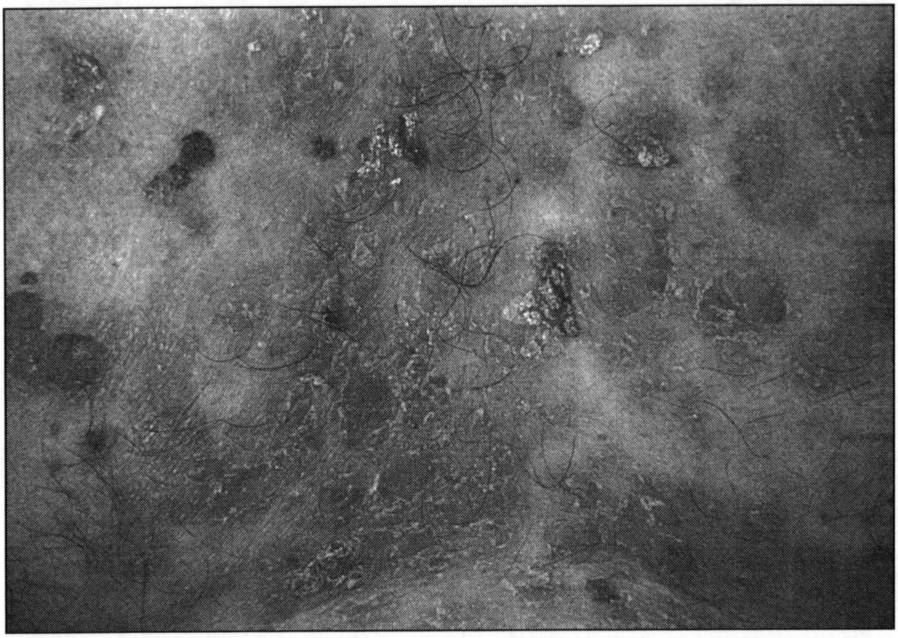

Courtesy of Centers for Disease Control and Prevention.

Hip fracture, replacement, or related injury

Hip fracture, replacement, or related injury

Assess and document the following each shift:

- Vital signs
- Appearance of operative site:
  - Describe condition of incision, including periphery of incision
  - Describe drainage, inflammation, nonhealing, other complications
  - Describe appearance of upper femur, including ecchymosis, edema, etc.
- Specific hip precautions used (document resident and staff teaching about precautions)
- Resident's position:
  - Describe the position
  - Document teaching about abduction pillow and avoiding crossing legs
- Presence of staples or sutures
- Color, temperature, and pulses distal to fracture
- Circulation in lower extremities; Check and document pedal pulse once daily
- Bed mobility; number of assistants
- Ability to transfer and bear weight, if any; number of assistants
- Activity tolerance
- What the resident can and cannot do without staff assistance

- Assistive devices, if any, for bed mobility and out-of-bed activities
- Presence of pain; describe assessment and nursing intervention
- Presence or absence of pressure ulcers
  - Check and document condition of heels every shift
- Measures to prevent skin breakdown, prevent pressure on heels and feet
- Presence or absence of contractures
- Rehabilitation documentation:
  - Ensure that nursing documentation does not contradict (e.g., if rehab states that resident transfers should be performed with one minimum assist, nursing documentation should be consistent—it shouldn't say "two maximum assistants")

Hypertension

Normal blood pressure, prehypertension, hypertension

	Blood pressure value (mmHg)		
Category	**Systolic**	*****	**Diastolic**
Normal	< 120	and	< 80
Prehypertension	120–139	or	< 80
High blood pressure			
Stage I hypertension	140–159	or	90–99
Stage II hypertension	160	or	100

Illness, general signs and symptoms (unknown etiology)

Take the following actions and document them each shift:

- Check for and consider recent laboratory values, if any.
- Evaluate new medications, adverse reactions, and side effects, if any.
- Monitor for signs/symptoms of dehydration or inadequate fluid intake (which causes hypovolemia):
  - Consider I&O monitoring
- Note any other changes from the resident's usual condition (i.e., what he or she is like on a normal day).
- If the resident is on warfarin, review and report most recent PT and INR, coagulation status, signs of internal bleeding.
- Determine whether other residents in the facility are being treated for or have recently experienced the same or similar signs and symptoms.
- Determine/study whether a relationship exists between other factors and the signs or symptoms the resident currently exhibits. For example, if the resident complains of nausea and has had vomiting or diarrhea, is there a relationship between the vomiting and medication administration time, initial doses of new medication, time of day, intake of certain foods or fluids, etc.?

Assess and document the following each shift:

- Changes in vital signs

- Chest pain
- Shortness of breath, difficulty breathing
- Initiate pulse oximetry, if short of breath
- Weakness or dizziness
- Headache
- Pain
- Nausea or vomiting
- Diarrhea
- Straining, constipation
- Cough
- Cyanosis or change in color
- Change in mental status
- Excessive thirst
- Frequent urination
- Lethargy
- Unusual drainage from a wound or body cavity

Incident report

The incident report for an accident or injury such as a fall should include the following information:

- Circumstances of the incident
- Date, time, and location of fall, and during which shift and on what unit the fall occurred
- Witnesses', staff members', and resident's accounts of the incident
- Interventions taken to care for the resident immediately after the incident
- Notifications made as a result of an incident
- Resident symptoms prior to the incident
- Vital signs and observations made after the incident
- Resident activity at the time of the incident
- Injuries/medical problems associated with the incident
- Environmental hazards or faulty equipment contributing to the incident
- Presence of any new incident risk factors
- Corrective actions taken to reduce the likelihood of another incident

The incident report is used to alert administrative personnel to problems, gather data, and provide quality assurance information for studies and statistics designed to reduce incidents and injuries. Avoid referring to the incident report elsewhere in your documentation. Referring to it makes it part of the medical record.

- Make sure all information on the incident report is legible.
- Avoid referring to incident reports to visitors, family members, and nonemployees.
- Avoid documenting your opinions or assumptions on the incident report. Document only facts.
- Avoid mentioning action to prevent recurrence in the incident report, such as having a piece of equipment repaired. However, if a single piece of potentially faulty equipment is mentioned in the incident report, it is appropriate to note immediate action taken. For example, you suspect a bed rail is not holding securely. Note that the resident has been placed in another bed until the bed rails can be inspected by maintenance.
- Never refer to an investigation or report to an insurance company on the incident report or medical record.
- Avoid making statements that place blame. Such statements are personal judgments. State the facts objectively.
- Complete the entire incident report during the shift on which the incident occurred.
- Use black ink.
- Document the particulars of the incident, including date, time, and notifications. Make sure the times are accurate.
- Avoid leaving blanks in data that may be questioned later. Be objective and avoid speculation. Describe what you saw or were told by the resident and witnesses.

- State the names of witnesses. Note that some facilities do not want addresses and phone numbers recorded, feeling that this provides helpful information to plaintiff attorneys. Follow your facility policy.
- Never ask a family member or visitor to complete or sign an incident report. Doing so entitles them to a copy of the report. If they insist on completing an incident report, do not provide a facility form. Have them write a statement on a piece of paper and sign it. Forward it to the appropriate administrative person.
- Never alter or falsify a medical record. Complete your documentation on incidents and injuries during the shift in which they occurred. Avoid late-entry charting, if possible.

Infection, general signs/ symptoms of (unknown etiology)

- Check for and consider recent laboratory values, if any.
- Evaluate new medications and side effects, if any.
- Monitor for signs/symptoms of dehydration or inadequate fluid intake (which causes hypovolemia):
- Consider I&O monitoring
- Note any other changes from the resident's usual condition (i.e., what he or she is like on a normal day).
- If the resident is on warfarin, review and report the most recent PT and INR, coagulation status, and signs of internal bleeding.
- Determine whether other residents in the facility are being treated for or have recently experienced the same or similar signs and symptoms.
- Determine/study whether a relationship exists between other factors and the signs or symptoms the resident currently exhibits. For example, if the resident complains of nausea or has had vomiting or diarrhea, is there a relationship between the vomiting and medication administration time, initial doses of new medication, time of day, intake of certain foods or fluids, etc.?

Assess and document the following each shift:

- Vital signs
- Elevated temperature

- Rapid pulse
- Rapid respirations
- Pulse oximetry, if short of breath
- Hypotension
- Fatigue
- New-onset mental confusion
- Sweating
- Chills
- Skin hot or cold to touch
- Skin flushed, red, gray, or blue
- Inflammation of skin as evidenced by redness, edema, heat, or pain
- Drainage from wounds or body cavities
- Abnormal drainage from any part of the body, such as mucus or pus

Rapid or new onset of four major syndromes often occur when infection is present in elderly persons. These may be the only signs or symptoms of acute illness:

- Confusion
- Falls
- Incontinence
- Immobility

Myocardial infarction

Take the following actions and document during each shift:

- Check for and consider recent laboratory values, if any
- Evaluate new medications and side effects, if any
- Note any other changes from the resident's usual condition (i.e., what he or she is like on a normal day)
- If the resident is on warfarin, review and report the most recent PT and INR, coagulation status, and signs of internal bleeding

Assess and document the following each shift:

- Vital signs
- Capillary refill
- Pulse oximetry
- Sudden-onset severe chest pain
- Pain—usually substernal; may radiate to shoulder, arm, teeth, jaw, or throat
- Apprehension, anxiety
- Pallor
- Diaphoresis
- Hypotension
- Rapid, weak, or irregular pulse

- Feeling faint
- Nausea/vomiting
- May have dyspnea, cyanosis, or cough
- Fever/abnormal vital signs

Note: Also see "chest pain" and "prerenal azotemia and acute renal failure"

Pain (etiology known or unknown)

Pain is *never* normal. All complaints of pain should be assessed by a nurse.

Assess and document the following evidence of pain each shift:

- Chest pain
- Pain that radiates
- Pain upon movement
- Pain during urination
- Pain when having a bowel movement

Type of pain	Description
Acute pain	Occurs suddenly and without warning. Acute pain is usually the result of tissue damage, caused by conditions such as injury or surgery. Typically, acute pain decreases over time, as healing takes place.
Persistent (chronic) pain	Persistent pain lasts longer than six months. (Another, older term for this type of pain is "chronic" pain). It may be intermittent or constant. Persistent pain may be caused by multiple medical conditions.
Phantom pain	Phantom pain occurs as a result of an amputation. The resident has had a body part, such as a leg, removed, but complains of pain in the toes. The pain is real, not imaginary.
Radiating pain	Radiating pain moves from the site of origin to other areas. For example, when a resident is having a heart attack, the pain may radiate from the chest to the jaw or arm.

Pain assessment

Assess and document the following one or more times each shift:

- If pain is present, determine the location, duration, character, and frequency
- If the resident is a new admission, obtain pain management history, if any
- If the resident is a new admission, obtain present pain management regimen, if any, and its effectiveness
- Teach resident about the use of a pain scale (figure 2.7) and have the resident select a scale that makes it easiest for him or her to communicate the level or intensity of pain:
  - Teach the resident about the pain scale when he or she is not in pain
  - Document the resident's preferred pain scale
  - Attempt to use the pain scale with cognitively impaired residents and evaluate their response (note that FACES or a picture scale may be effective)
- Evaluate pain quality
- Determine pain intensity (by use of pain rating scale, if possible)
- Assess for radiation, if any
- Determine whether there are variations or patterns of pain
- Assess for aggravating and alleviating factors
- Evaluate the effect of pain on activities of daily living, sleep, appetite, relationships, emotions, concentration, etc.

Figure 2.7

EXAMPLES OF PAIN SCALES

The Wong-Baker FACES pain rating scale, is a simple 0–5 scale that was published in Wong, D.L., *Whaley and Wong's Nursing Care of Infants and Children.*

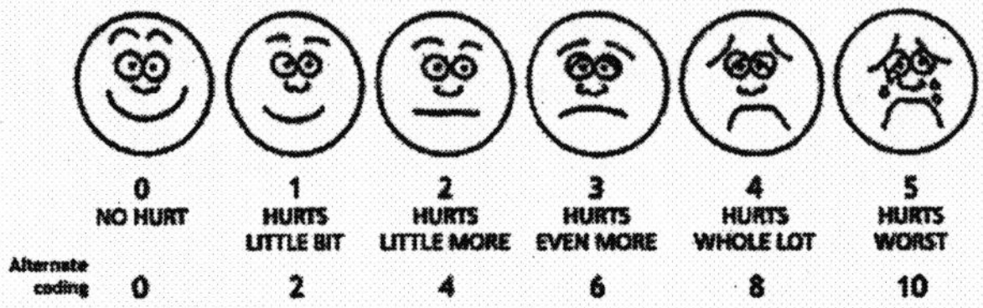

The FACES scale works well for many elderly residents, including those with cognitive impairment.

Source: FACES Pain Rating Scale from Hockenberry MJ, Wilson D, Winkelstein ML: Wong's Essentials of Pediatric Nursing, ed. 7, St. Louis, 2005, p. 1259. Used with permission. Copyright Mosby.

Figure 2.7 (cont.)

Examples of Pain Scales (cont.)

Numeric pain scales, in which 0 indicates no pain, and 10 describes severe pain.

B.

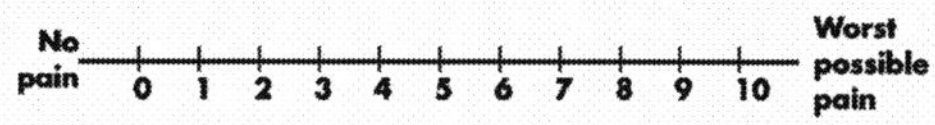

C.

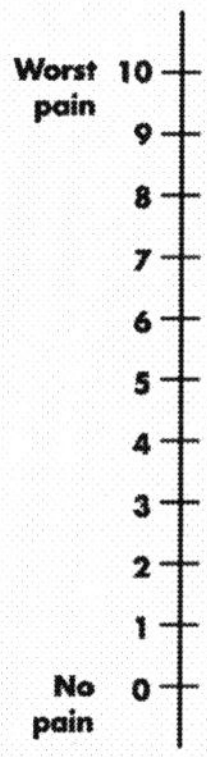

Example verbal pain scales

D.

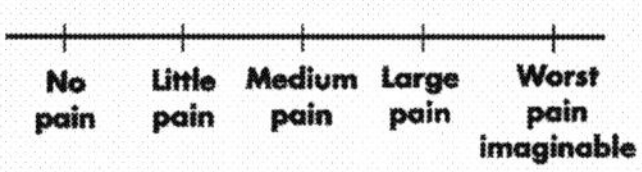

E.

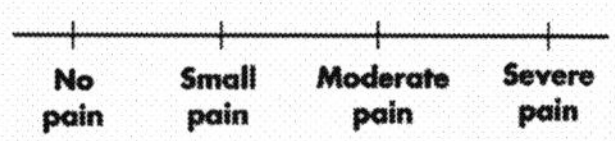

F.

SERIOUS PAIN
MODERATE PAIN
LITTLE PAIN
NO PAIN

G.

TOO MUCH HURT
LOTS OF HURT
LITTLE HURT
NO HURT

Residents have varying pain scale preferences.
Ask the resident which pain scale helps best describe the pain intensity.

- Perform a physical assessment and direct observation/examination of the site of the pain
- Evaluate side effects of analgesic medications, if applicable
- Evaluate response to analgesia and other forms of treatment, if applicable
- Monitor for and document any of the following nonverbal signs of pain (also consider these in cognitively impaired residents):
  - Behavior changes
  - Facial expressions
  - Body language
  - Verbal indications of pain (such as moaning)
  - Moaning, groaning, grunting, gasping, etc.
  - Grimacing
  - Guarded positioning
  - Withdrawing from touch
  - Restlessness
  - Irregular respirations
  - Intermittent breath holding
  - Dilated pupils
  - Sweating
  - Favoring one extremity
  - Irritability
  - Withdrawal (emotional)

- Fatigue
- Anorexia
- Behavior that appears opposite of normal
- A noisy resident becomes quiet
- A resident who rambles and does not make sense suddenly describes his or her pain
- A quiet resident becomes belligerent or combative
- An outgoing resident cries or withdraws
- An active resident is motionless for a long period of time

• Document/describe nursing actions and intervention:
  - Document the pain rating scale selected by the resident
  - Describe the resident's response to nursing intervention
  - Document healthcare provider and responsible party notifications

• Update the care plan for new pain; schedule for next care conference meeting

• Note the resident's preferred pain assessment scale and the frequency of pain assessments

• Initiate 24-hour monitoring; if short-acting analgesics are given or the resident is on a new pain regimen, pain assessment should be frequent—every two to three hours

Nursing responsibilities for managing pain

The goal of pain management is to eliminate the cause of the pain, provide analgesia, or both. Avoid assuming that because a resident cannot express or respond to pain that it does not exist. Manage pain by eliminating or controlling the source. Provide analgesia as needed and appropriate.

Nursing responsibilities for assessing, managing, and evaluating effectiveness of pain management include the following:

- Determining the nature of the pain and its impact on the resident
- Identifying factors that affect the resident's perception and expression of pain
- Determining when to administer analgesics
- Deciding which analgesic to administer, if more than one is ordered
- Determining the dose of analgesic medication to administer, if a range is prescribed
- Evaluating the effectiveness of the analgesic
- Assessing for and managing side effects of the medication
- Determining why the analgesic was ineffective, if applicable
- Determining the need to change the dose, timing, or medication and reporting this information to the healthcare provider
- Using nursing interventions to promote comfort and relieve pain

- Making sure the plan of care describes pain assessment and management
- Documenting pain assessment and intervention noted herein to reflect use of the nursing process

Peripheral vascular disease: Leg ulcer comparison

Arterial leg ulcers	Diabetic leg ulcers	Venous leg ulcers
Causative or predisposing factors		
• Diabetes mellitus • Advanced age (usually > 45; often elderly) • Peripheral vascular disease • Arteriosclerosis • Atherosclerosis • History of intermittent claudication	• Diabetes mellitus with peripheral neuropathy • Hyperglycemia	• Valvular incompetence in lower legs • Venous hypertension • Pooling of blood in lower legs • History of phlebitis (DVT or thrombosis) • Previous history of leg ulcers • Obesity • Advanced age

Arterial leg ulcers	Diabetic leg ulcers	Venous leg ulcers
Common locations of ulcers		
• Between or on tips of toes • Over the knuckle area of toes (phalangeal heads) • On tips of heels • On lower legs • On bony prominences of foot and ankle; commonly on lateral malleolus, rarely over medial malleolus of ankle • On any area subject to rubbing from shoes or clothing • On any area subjected to trauma	• Under the heels • Over the knuckle area of toes (phalangeal heads) • Between or on tips of toes • On the balls of the feet • Over metatarsal heads • On bony prominences or areas exposed to pressure	• On ankles • Anywhere on lower extremities; most common is middle of the lower leg, where pressure is greatest

Arterial leg ulcers	Diabetic leg ulcers	Venous leg ulcers
Appearance and characteristics of lower legs and feet		
• Skin dry, thin • Skin appears "tight" and shiny • Hair loss on foot and ankle • Toenails thick • Pallor of lower legs when elevated • Red color (rubra) of lower legs when down • Loss of subcutaneous fat, atrophy • Cyanosis • Coolness to touch, decreased skin temperature • Decreased or absent pulses • Capillary refill delayed (> three seconds) • Pain when walking and, in later stages, at rest; pain may be intense when limb is elevated	• Sensation diminished or absent in feet • Decreased or absent ability to feel temperature changes • Deformities of feet • Palpable pulses • Skin warm to touch • Loss of fatty tissue, atrophy of subcutaneous fat • Resident complains of paresthesia ("pins and needles" sensation) • Ulcer probably painful • Pain may be relieved by ambulation	• Edema, firm to touch, may be pitting • Palpable pulses • Dilated veins/varicosities visible on surface of skin • Thin, dry skin • History of healed ulcers • Area around wound hyperpigmented (highly colored; blue or brown color) • Rashes or dermatitis • Fibrosis • Resident may complain of throbbing pain, which worsens at night or during activity

Arterial leg ulcers	Diabetic leg ulcers	Venous leg ulcers
Appearance of ulcerated area		
• Wound margins are well defined, regular, even • Necrotic tissue present • Gangrene possible; resident risk is high • Wound bed white or pale in color • Blanched or purple skin surrounding wound • Severe pain; decreases with leg dependency and increases with cool environment, activity, or leg elevation • Cellulitis, infection • Minimal drainage • Heals slowly	• Wound margins even and regular • Wound bed deep • Infection, cellulitis • May have osteomyelitis • Small to moderate amount of drainage • Sensation diminished or absent • Skin may appear brown in color • May have calloused area around ulcer	• Irregular shape • Ulcer is superficial, flat—a shallow crater • May be covered with yellow, moist tissue • Red-brown or blue color surrounding the wound • Usually not painful; pain increases with leg dependency and decreases with cool temperature, leg elevation, and activity • Moderate to heavy drainage • May have scaly, dry rash surrounding wound • Surrounding tissue fibrotic • Resident may complain of severe pruritus • Edema • Exudate

Pressure ulcer(s)

Pressure ulcer care begins with accurate wound assessment and healthcare provider notification. The treatment product selected is determined largely by the wound characteristics identified in the nursing assessment, so accuracy is critical.

Assess the ulcer initially, and document the following:

- Location.
- Stage.
- Size (note that pressure ulcers are measured using metric measurements: length x width x depth; 1 in. = 2.54 cm; 1 cm = 0.3937 in.):
    - Length—measurement in head-to-toe direction
    - Width—measurement in hip-to-hip direction
    - Depth—measurement of deepest visible portion of wound bed
- Presence of sinus tracts (tunneling), undermining (use the clock system to document location; i.e., tunnel at 9:00).
- Exudate, presence or absence of odor and unusual drainage, including the following types of drainage:
    - Sanguineous—thin, bright red
    - Serosanguineous—thin, watery, pale red to pink
    - Serous—thin, watery, clear

  - Purulent—thick or thin, commonly yellow, but may be opaque tan to yellow
  - Foul purulent—thick opaque yellow to green with offensive odor
- Amount of drainage:
  - None—wound tissue is dry
  - Scant—no measurable drainage, but wound tissue is moist
  - Small—wound tissue is very moist, with drainage on < 25% of the dressing
  - Moderate—wound tissue is wet, drainage involves 25%–75% of the dressing
  - Large—wound tissue is filled with fluid and involves > 75% of the dressing
  - Copious—wound tissue saturated and dressing is saturated; may be leaking and does not contain drainage
- Presence or absence of necrosis (describe):
  - Eschar is commonly dark in color and has a thick, hard consistency; note whether loose or adherent
  - Slough is usually lighter in color and has a thin, stringy consistency
- Presence or absence of granulation tissue and epithelialization:
  - Granulation tissue is usually beefy red, granular, or bubbly in appearance
  - Differentiate granulation tissue from a smooth, red wound bed
- Describe color of tissue (pale pink to dusky red):
  - Epithelialization
  - Can be deep pink, then progress to pearly pink/light purple from the edges in full thickness wound

  - May form islands in the wound base with a superficial wound
  - Describe using percentage or clock system

- Appearance of wound margins:
  - Firmness
  - Intact or nonintact
  - Presence or absence of edema
  - Color

- Other abnormalities, such as rashes or pain, irregular border.

- Evaluate the ulcer at the time of each treatment. If the condition of the resident or wound deteriorates, immediately reevaluate the treatment plan and contact the healthcare provider.

- Reassess the ulcer at least weekly, any time there is a change, or according to facility policy. Consider a policy requiring descriptive documentation of the ulcer before a resident leaves the facility (e.g., for pass, hospitalization, etc.) and immediately upon return. Document the results of all ulcer assessments in the medical record.

- If no progress in healing is noted in two weeks, reevaluate the adequacy of the treatment plan, as well as adherence to this plan. Modify as needed. Notify the healthcare provider.

- Individualize treatment to the wound. If a debriding agent is used on the ulcer, discontinue it as soon as necrotic tissue is removed. Protect the healthy skin surrounding the ulcer when debriding agents are used.

- Assess the resident:

- Complete nursing assessment, including history and physical examination
- Presence or absence of complicating conditions
- Nutritional assessment (dietitian consult on next visit)
- Hydration assessment (nursing assessment immediately pending dietitian evaluation)
- Consider I&O monitoring and calorie count to gather data pending dietitian visit
- Pain assessment
- Psychosocial assessment

- Correct nutritional deficiencies. Notify the dietitian about the ulcer and request his or her evaluation and recommendations.
- Correct fluid deficiencies. Ask the dietitian to calculate the resident's minimum fluid needs. Record this number. Consider instituting I&O monitoring to ensure that the resident's fluid needs are met. Evaluate the resident's total fluid intake each day for adequacy (compare with dietitian's calculations, which may be listed on the care plan).
- Provide pain management by eliminating mechanical sources of pain and providing analgesia. Assess the resident frequently, using a pain scale if possible. Be sure premedication is given prior to dressing changes and treatments.
- Arrange interventions to meet psychosocial needs and goals.
- Manage tissue loads. The goal of load management is to create an environment that enhances soft tissue viability and promotes healing of the pressure ulcer(s).

Use

- positioning techniques and support surfaces
- positioning devices
- written schedules

- Avoid positioning residents on a pressure ulcer, as well as on donut-type devices.
- Use devices, pillows, or foam to elevate the heels off the bed and keep knees and ankles from touching or rubbing together.
- Maintain the head of the bed at the lowest degree medically necessary.
- A resident should avoid sitting if he or she has an ulcer on a sitting surface.
- Move a sitting resident at least once an hour.
- Institute preventive measures to prevent additional ulcers from developing.
- Frequently evaluate the treatment and modify the plan of care.

Adapted from U.S. Department of Health and Human Services, eds. 1994. Pressure Ulcer Treatment. *Rockville, MD: Agency for Health Care Policy and Research.*

Determining whether a pressure ulcer infection is present

A colonized wound will heal. An infected wound will not heal. If the ulcer is not healing, suspect infection.

Many tools are available to help you determine whether wound infection is present. In addition to evaluating the appearance of the wound, look at the whole picture. Assess the resident:

- Evaluate the vital signs:
  - Does the resident have a fever?
  - Are the vital signs normal or abnormal?
- Evaluate the wound:
  - Is the wound red or swollen?
  - Is bone exposed? (This is an indication of potential osteomyelitis and requires further diagnostic testing.)
- Evaluate drainage:
  - Is there purulent drainage or a foul odor?
- Evaluate the periphery:
  - Palpate the tissue. Is the area surrounding the wound warm to the touch compared with other nearby skin or skin on the opposite extremity?
- Assess pain:
  - Does the resident have new or increased pain in the ulcer?
- Consider additional laboratory testing, such as
  - white blood cell count (WBC)
  - erythrocyte sedimentation rate (ESR)
  - C-reactive protein
  - deep tissue culture (not swab)
  - blood culture
  - x-ray examination nuclear medicine testing (gallium, technetium, and indium scans)

- Evaluate the clinical picture carefully. For example, an elevated WBC without the clinical appearance of infection could indicate an infection elsewhere in the body. However, the resident may have no systemic signs of infection. Good assessment skills are essential in identifying wound infection. The only indication of infection may be poor wound healing. Alert nursing personnel will promptly identify the problem when wound healing stalls, inform the healthcare provider, and initiate a course of nursing action.
- If a wound bed infection is present and the resident has no signs or symptoms of systemic infection, consider using topical therapy such as silver or an antibiotic cream or ointment. Oral and parenteral antibiotics may be ineffective because the tissue is devitalized and avascular. Reserve the oral and parenteral antibiotics for systemic infection, cellulitis, sepsis, or osteomyelitis.

Radiation therapy

Assess and document the following each shift:

- Vital signs
- Lung sounds
- Bowel sounds
- Appearance of skin at site of radiation, including erythema, pruritus, edema, desquamation of skin (dry or moist), color and appearance of area, pain
- Presence or absence of nausea/vomiting
- Complaints of anorexia
- Presence or absence of dysphagia
- Presence or absence of malaise or fatigue
- Presence or absence of hair loss
- Change in voiding pattern
- Psychological response to condition

Renal failure, acute prerenal azotemia

- Check for and consider recent laboratory values, if any
- Evaluate new medications and side effects, if any
- Note any other changes from the resident's usual condition (i.e., what he or she is like on a normal day)
- If the resident is on warfarin, review and report the most recent PT and INR, coagulation status, and signs of internal bleeding

Assess and document the following each shift:

- Vital signs
- Elevated blood pressure
- Reduced urine production; little or no urine produced
- Confusion, decreased alertness, progressively worsening
- Pallor
- Rapid pulse
- Dry mouth
- Thirst
- Edema
- Abdominal pain
- May have increased urination at night

- The resident may have signs or symptoms of infection elsewhere in the body

Late signs and symptoms include the following:

- Low blood pressure
- Signs of shock
- Decreased pulse pressure

Note and act on any of the following abnormal laboratory values:

- Elevated BUN
- Elevated creatinine
- Increased BUN/creatinine ratio
- Gradual serum potassium increase
- Low urine sodium
- Urine creatinine to serum creatinine ratio is high
- Increased osmolality and specific gravity of urine
- Monitor for signs/symptoms of dehydration, inadequate fluid intake (which causes hypovolemia):
    - Consider *strict* I&O monitoring
    - Complete narrative nursing evaluation of results of I&O monitoring every 24 hours

Renal failure, chronic

Residents receiving dialysis treatment for ESRD

- Check for and consider recent laboratory values, if any
- Evaluate new medications and side effects, if any
- Monitor for signs/symptoms of dehydration, inadequate fluid intake (which causes hypovolemia):
  - Residents on dialysis should be on I&O monitoring; consider changing to *strict* I&O monitoring
- Note any other changes from the resident's usual condition (i.e., what he or she is like on a normal day)
- If the resident is on warfarin, review and report the most recent PT and INR, coagulation status, and signs of internal bleeding

Assess and document the following each shift:

- Weigh the resident daily, or according to healthcare provider order, and document
  - if weekly weights are ordered, obtain the weight immediately upon return from dialysis treatments (after excess fluid has been removed)
- *Immediately upon return* from dialysis, monitor the resident's
  - general appearance
  - neurological status (particularly the level of consciousness)

- cardiac and respiratory status
- gastrointestinal status
- vital signs—monitor blood pressure closely until stable; if resident is hypotensive or complains of dizziness, supervise activity and provide safety measures until blood pressure returns to normal (resident may be weak or dizzy related to the amount of fluid removed from the body)

- Regularly auscultate or palpate the shunt through which dialysis is administered for the presence of a thrill (vibration) or bruit (sound) to ensure that the shunt is patent:
  - Assess peripheral circulation and neurological status distal to the shunt (impaired peripheral blood flow may result as the shunt bypasses or diverts blood from the distal anatomy)
- If resident is noncompliant with fluid or dietary restrictions, note measures taken
- Monitor and evaluate/assess daily *strict* I&O
- Monitor for and identify patterns of behavior leading to problems with fluid balance and develop a plan of care to address these patterns and eliminate the problem
- Assess regularly for clinical signs and symptoms of congestive heart failure and fluid overload
- Monitor for and document edema
- Monitor for and document signs of fluid and electrolyte imbalance, including abnormal laboratory values, motor weakness, changes in skin, muscle twitching, bruising, and leg cramps

- Document/describe nursing actions and intervention:
  - Describe the resident's response to nursing intervention
  - Document healthcare provider and responsible party notifications
- Update care plan for special monitoring and abnormalities
- Initiate 24-hour monitoring
- Monitor for signs and symptoms of dehydration each shift (the most common cause of prerenal azotemia/early renal failure), including
  - reduced urine production; little or no urine produced
  - confusion, decreased alertness, progressively worsening
  - pallor
  - rapid pulse
  - dry mouth
  - thirst
  - edema
  - abdominal pain
  - may have increased urination at night
  - may have signs or symptoms of infection elsewhere in the body
  - low blood pressure
  - signs of shock
  - decreased pulse pressure
- Monitor the resident each shift, or more often, for the following signs and symptoms:

- Inadequate urinary output compared with intake; less than 500 cc of output in 24 hours is an ominous sign—notify healthcare provider promptly
- Elevated blood pressure
- Edema of the hands and feet
- Edema about the eyes and face
- Pain in the kidney area
- Difficulty urinating or burning upon urination
- More frequent urination during the night
- Passage of bloody or cola-colored urine
- Abnormal pulse and respirations
- Delirium, change in mental status
- Nausea and/or vomiting
- Presence or absence of uremic frost on the skin
- Abnormal color, odor, or appearance of urine; presence of sediment
- Loss of appetite
- Intense itching on skin surface (related to excretion of toxins)
- Thirst
- Twitching
- Bone pain

• Each shift, assess the resident's
  - cardiac and respiratory status
  - neurologic and musculoskeletal status

Restraint order (new)

- Monitor and assess for signs and symptoms of acute illness or delirium affecting behavior
- Document/describe nursing actions and intervention to avoid restraint use:
  - Describe the resident's response to nursing intervention
- Obtain a healthcare provider's order for the use of restraints; the order should include, and you should document, the following prerequisites for restraint use:
  - Type of restraint
  - Reason for restraint
  - Time restraint is to be applied
  - Release of restraint (you may write "release according to facility policies")
- Document explanation given to the resident, family, or legal guardian for restraint use:
  - Document the reason if the resident was not involved in the explanation about restraint use
  - Obtain written consent for restraint use
- Assess and document the reason for using restraints
- Assess the resident to determine whether less restrictive measures can be used to keep the resident safe and document the results of your assessment, including

- safety of the resident or other residents
- behavior changes related to impaired thought processes
- severe anxiety, depression, or other psychological conditions
- the need for physical immobility, body positioning, or other needs
- resistance to or refusal of treatment, medication, nourishment, or other care
- psychotropic drug use
- emergency circumstances necessitating restraint, if any
- declines in functional status related to loss of mobility, balance, or muscle tone; increased agitation; reduced social contact; hearing/vision impairment; communication deficits
- acute or chronic illness progression

- Document types of devices that have been tried to keep the resident safe, alternatives to the devices, and their effectiveness, including
  - behavior management program
  - reminder-type devices (e.g., lap buddy, personal alarm, etc.)
  - self-releasing devices
  - devices that prevent rising (e.g., wedge cushion, beanbag, etc.)
  - scheduled regimen for toileting and exercise
- Update the care plan to reflect the restraint orders:
  - Schedule resident for next care conference to discuss new restraint orders
- Ensure that the restraint applied to the resident is the proper type and size and is applied correctly; list this information on the care plan

- Monitor the resident for safety while he or she is using restraints and document the monitoring and results
- Prepare a form for documentation of q15–30-minute visual check and q2-hour release
- Reassess restraint use quarterly, or more often, if necessary, and document the effects of the restraint, including
  - physical, mental, and psychosocial side effects
  - whether functioning is improved, declined, or maintained
  - whether the restraint can be reduced to a less restrictive device during the quarterly reassessment
- Document healthcare provider and responsible party notifications
- Initiate 24-hour monitoring because of new restraint order

Note: Also see documentation guidelines for behavior.

Scabies

Scabies is an infestation or parasitic disease of the skin caused by the mite *Sarcoptes scabiei*. The mite is primarily transmitted by direct skin-to-skin contact. Transmission is often through person-to-person contact or by indirect contact with contaminated

- undergarments
- bedclothes
- linens
- cracks in mattresses
- blankets
- pillows
- clothing
- lotions and creams
- gait belts
- upholstered furniture

Incubation period

In persons without previous exposure, the incubation period is two to six weeks before onset of itching (figure 2.8). Persons who have been previously infested are much more sensitive and usually develop symptoms one to four days after reexposure.

Figure 2.8

The life cycle of the scabies mite.

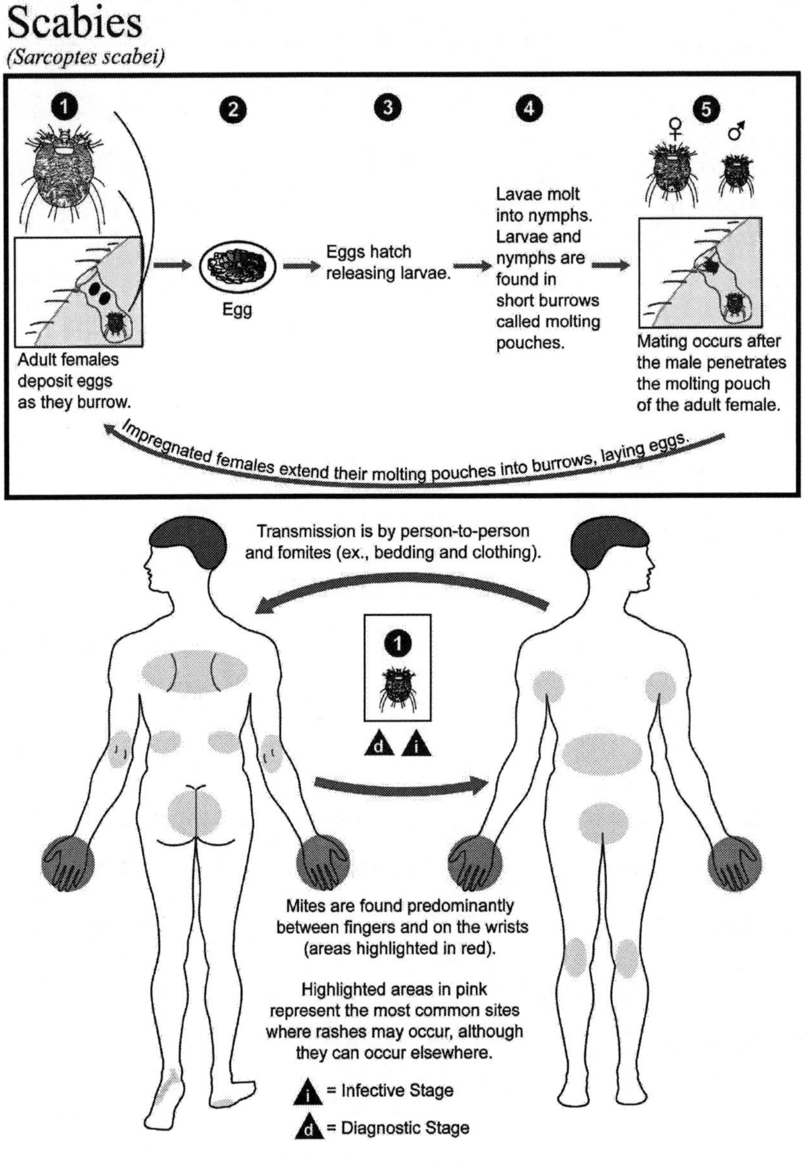

Courtesy of Centers for Disease Control and Prevention.

Be suspicious if residents and employees develop a rash and itching in a short period of time. Scabies is fairly common in long-term care, but the diagnosis of the condition is almost always delayed for a prolonged period of time. Scabies can imitate and may be misdiagnosed as many other skin conditions, including allergy, insect bites, hives, eczema, folliculitis, contact or atopic dermatitis, impetigo, rosacea, psoriasis, lymphoma, and drug reactions.

Clinical manifestations

- Determine whether other residents in the facility are being treated for or have recently experienced the same or similar signs and symptoms.
- Following the incubation period
    - the resident will complain of severe itching
    - he or she may scratch until the skin bleeds
    - the itching will not respond to topical moisturizers or antihistamines
    - the itching sensation often worsens when the resident is in bed
    - scratching may cause an infection, worsening the condition and contributing to misdiagnosis
- The resident develops rash-like areas on the skin that may consist of papules, vesicles, or tiny linear lesions. The most common locations are
    - the webs of the fingers (figure 2.9a) and following the course of blood vessels on the hands (figure 2.9b)
    - inside the wrists
    - outside the elbows
    - in the underarm, waist, and breast and nipple areas (figure 2.10)

Figure 2.9a

The pimple-like rash in the webbing between the fingers of this adult's hand was due to *Sarcoptes scabiei var. hominis*. Scabies is a highly contagious infestation of the skin caused by a mite affecting humans and animals. Scabies is usually transmitted by intimate interpersonal contact, often sexual in nature, but transmission through casual contact can occur as well.

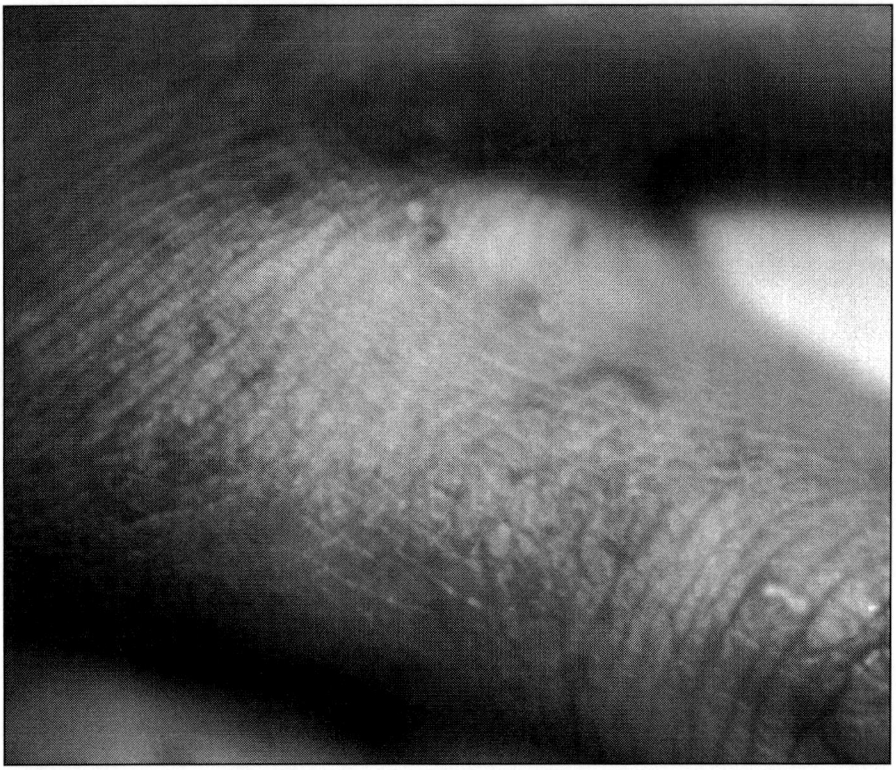

Courtesy of Centers for Disease Control and Prevention.

Figure 2.9b

This patient's hand reveals a scabies infestation of the mite species *Sarcoptes scabiei var. hominis*. The scabies rash manifests itself as pimple-like eruptions, especially within the webbing between the fingers; the skin folds on the wrist, elbow, or knee; the penis; the breast; and the shoulder blades.

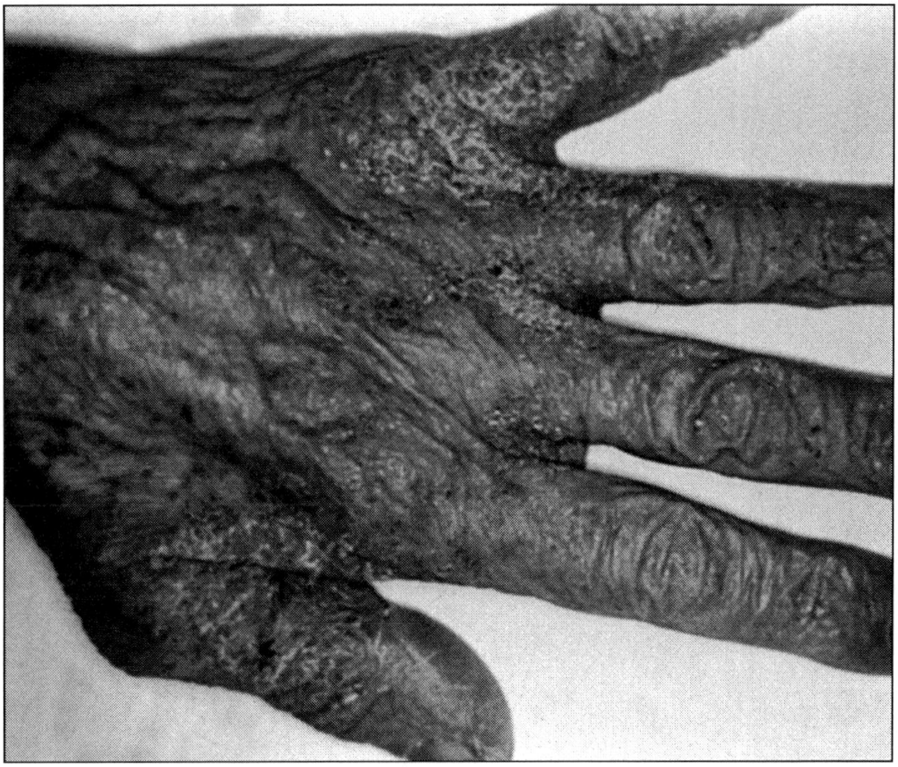

Courtesy of Centers for Disease Control and Prevention.

Figure 2.10

Symptoms of scabies include pimple-like irritations, burrows, or rash of the skin, especially the webbing between the fingers; the skin folds on the wrist, elbow, or knee; the penis; the breast; or the shoulder blades. Other symptoms include intense itching, especially at night and over most of the body. Sores on the body result from scratching. These sores sometimes become infected with bacteria.

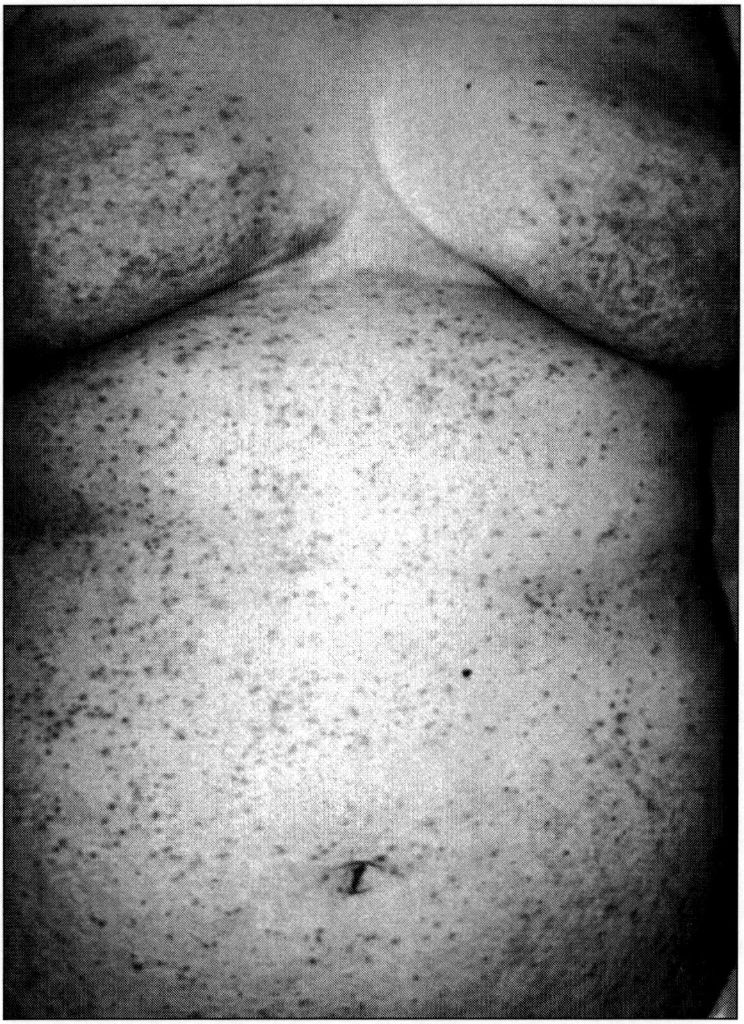

Courtesy of Centers for Disease Control and Prevention.

- Rash is common around the knees, lower buttocks, and the genital area in males.
- Norwegian scabies cause scaling of the skin on the hands and feet.
- Skin that has been exposed to moisture may be more heavily involved.
- Skin may appear excoriated.
- Norwegian scabies is an unusual presentation involving hyperkeratinization and crusting of the skin—causing a "scaly skin" appearance:
  - Persons with atypical or crusted scabies harbor hundreds to millions of mites in multiple skin burrows or in layers of crusted skin lesions and are highly contagious. By contrast, approximately 50 mites reside in the burrows of typical scabies.

Treatment

- Involved residents and staff should be treated with a scabicide during the same time frame.
- Depending on the treatment product used, an additional application may be recommended. *Note that Lindane is not recommended for treatment of elderly persons.*
- The period of communicability may persist until all infested residents and staff are treated.
- Following treatment, residents/staff may resume routine activities. Itching and rash may persist for up to a month
- Residents are usually in contact precautions for 24 hours; all linen, bedding, clothing, and furnishings in room should be thoroughly laundered or cleaned.

Scabies: Special assessment and recordkeeping

If scabies is diagnosed, the infection control nurse will develop a list of every individual who has had direct contact with the affected person. If many people are infested, start a separate contact list for each. Include roommates and employees who are no longer at the facility. Document

- employee or resident name
- room number
- date symptoms began
- results of diagnostic testing
- date of treatment/retreatment, and results

You should also

- evaluate the infested persons' activities for the past four weeks and identify others who have potentially been exposed.
- identify staff who have cared for the resident. This may include hospital and ambulance personnel, hospice workers, and volunteers. Determine whether these individuals are symptomatic.
- notify the resident's family and visitors.
- check all nursing units to determine if individuals there are also symptomatic.
- identify residents and staff needing treatment. Treat symptomatic persons first. Determine whether family members of staff are symptomatic.
- document appearance, location, pruritus, and other signs of infestation weekly (or more often) after treatment.

Seizures

Type of seizure	Signs of seizure activity	Comments
Generalized tonic-clonic seizure (Grand mal seizure)	May be preceded by an aura. Loss of consciousness, convulsive activity, characterized by rigid stiffening of muscles and jerking movement of the arms and legs. Saliva runs from the mouth. Resident's color may change because of lack of oxygen. Incontinence of bowel and bladder.	Usually lasts three to four minutes. The resident may be very tired after the seizure and have a headache. The resident may be mentally confused, have slurred speech, and be very weak. The resident will not remember the seizure.

Type of seizure	Signs of seizure activity	Comments
Absence seizure (Petit mal seizure)	Staring, blinking, or stopping what the resident is doing. The resident may stare blankly. One muscle group may twitch or jerk. The seizure begins without warning and consists of a period of unconsciousness in which the resident blinks rapidly, stares blankly, breathes rapidly, or makes chewing movements. The seizure lasts two to 10 seconds, then ends abruptly. The resident usually resumes normal activity immediately. Because these seizures are mild, they may be unnoticed. Children with absence seizures may have learning problems if the seizures are not identified and treated.	Petit mal seizures usually last less than a minute but may occur many times a day.

Type of seizure	Signs of seizure activity	Comments
Simple-partial (Jacksonian seizure)	Involves only part of the brain and can be a sensation or feeling with no abnormal muscle activity. If muscle spasms occur, they begin with spasms of the face, hands, or feet. Starts at one extremity, such as an arm or leg, and progressively moves upward on that side of the body.	May spread to other areas in the brain, resulting in a grand mal seizure.
Complex-partial (Psychomotor)	Abnormal acts, irrational behavior, or loss of judgment due to a temporary change in consciousness. Automatic behavior, such as typing or eating, may continue normally. The resident may uncontrollably smack his or her lips, wander aimlessly, or uncontrollably twitch part of his or her body.	Usually lasts only a few seconds. The resident usually does not remember the seizure.

Seizures

Type of seizure	Signs of seizure activity	Comments
Myoclonic	Consists of one or more myoclonic jerks. The resident remains conscious but cannot control the muscle movement.	The resident is aware that an extremity is jerking but is unable to stop it. The resident remains conscious throughout and can remember the seizure activity.
Status epilepticus	Multiple seizures occurring simultaneously with no break between seizures. When this seizure begins, the resident cries out, then falls to the floor. The muscles stiffen (tonic phase), then the extremities begin to jerk and twitch (clonic phase). The resident may lose bladder control. Consciousness returns slowly. After this seizure, the resident may feel tired, or be confused and disoriented. This may last from a few minutes to several hours or days. The resident may fall asleep, or gradually become less confused until full consciousness returns.	Status epilepticus may be precipitated by sudden withdrawal of antiseizure medications, fever, and infection. This type of seizure is dangerous and can lead to decreased mental function, neurological impairment, and death.

- Note time that the seizure started and stopped
- Describe seizure activity
- Check vital signs
- Check capillary refill
- Complete neuro checks
- Assess Glasgow Coma Scale
- Initiate pulse oximetry immediately after seizure
- Check for new focal deficits, such as CVA/TIA
- Note whether resident has seizure diagnosis
- Note whether it is a new-onset or first-time seizure
- Assess change in mental status
- Evaluate for loss of consciousness
- Determine whether the resident experienced an aura
- Fingerstick blood sugar
- Monitor intensively for recurrence
- Describe post-ictal state

Sepsis, urosepsis

- Check for and consider recent laboratory values, if any
- Evaluate new medications and side effects, if any
- Monitor for signs/symptoms of dehydration and inadequate fluid intake (which causes hypovolemia):
  - Consider I&O monitoring
- Note any other changes from the resident's usual condition (i.e., what he or she is like on a normal day)

Note: Signs and symptoms depend on how far advanced the condition is when it is identified.

Assess and document the following each shift:

- Vital signs
- Fever (early sign)
- Tachycardia (early sign)
- Hyperventilation (early sign)
- Warm, dry, flushed skin (early sign)
- Hypotension (late sign)
- Hypothermia (late sign)
- Hypoxia (late sign)

- Rapid, shallow respirations progressing to dyspnea, respiratory distress (late sign)
- Tachycardia, pulse weak and thready (late sign)
- Cool, clammy skin (late sign)
- Pulmonary edema (late sign)
- Crackles in lungs (late sign)
- Oliguria (late sign)
- Marked mental decline progressing to unresponsiveness (late sign)

Note: Also see "Prerenal azotemia and acute renal failure."

Definitions

- *Sepsis* is a severe infection caused by the presence of toxins; it can occur anywhere in the body. Hypothermia is a cardinal sign of sepsis in the elderly.
- *Septicemia* is a systemic infection in the bloodstream. Bacteria multiply and release toxins into the blood stream, which spreads the toxins throughout the system. This condition was formerly called "blood poisoning."
- *Septic Shock* is the outcome of serious infection. It is caused by serious infection, usually those caused by Gram negative bacteria. Like other forms of shock, we cannot predict exactly when it will occur. Also, like other types of shock, it reaches a point when it becomes irreversible. One goal of treatment for infection is to prevent septic shock. Onset of septic shock is heralded by hypothermia, low blood pressure, rapid pulse, inadequate tissue perfusion, hemodynamic changes, and compromised organ function.
- *Urosepsis* is a sepsis caused by a urinary tract infection or a catheter.

Skin-tear assessment and classification

The *Payne-Martin Classification System*[1] is being used to successfully classify and treat skin tears. Research to validate this tool is ongoing, but the results in clinical practice are very promising. The classification system is as follows:

- Category I—Edges of the skin tear can be approximated (within 1 mm) with no tissue loss:
  - Type A: Linear
  - Type B: Flap
- Category II—Varying amounts of tissue loss:
  - Type A: Scant tissue loss < 25%
  - Type B: Moderate to large tissue loss > 25%
- Category III—Complete tissue loss; epidermal flap is absent

Treatment

The goal of treatment is to promote healing with the least amount of trauma possible, minimize pain, and prevent infection. No single research-based treatment exists, so most facilities develop their own protocol based on existing research. Treatment typically consists of the following:

- Gently clean the skin tear with normal saline or pH-neutral cleanser, according to facility policy.
- Allow the area to air dry or gently pat it dry.

- Assess and stage the skin tear. Measure size, if this is your facility policy.
- Approximate the flap. Avoid stretching the skin. Use an applicator moistened in normal saline to cover the wound and approximate the edges, if necessary. Avoid folding the skin over onto itself, because this will prevent adherence.
- Apply Steri-Strips, if necessary, for Category I and Category IIA skin tears. Allow them to fall off on their own as the wound heals. Once applied, do not attempt to remove them.
- Apply petroleum-based ointment, hydrogel, or a moist, nonadherent dressing, according to facility policy.
- Select a dressing based on wound size, characteristics, your assessment, and facility policy. Many products can be used to promote a healing environment, including nonadherent dressings, hydrogels, petroleum-based gauze, collagen dressings, foams, transparent films, hydrocolloids, and Steri-Strips.

Category I and II skin tears:

- Cover with
  - transparent film dressing if the skin has good turgor and there is little to no edema. Change every three to seven days as long as integrity is maintained and the fluid that collects underneath remains clear.
  - nonadherent dressing and wrap if the skin has poor turgor or there is edema present. Apply topical antimicrobial ointment if desired. Change outer dressing daily. Secure nonadherent dressings with a bandage or gauze wrap, if possible. Avoid tape.

Category III skin tears:

- Trim any remnants of skin that are avascular (nonviable), if permitted by facility policy and nurse practice act.

- Cover with
  - hydrocolloid if the skin has good turgor and there is little edema. Change every three to seven days.
  - topical antimicrobial ointment/silver products and nonadherent dressing, then wrap if the skin has poor turgor, or if edema or high amount of drainage is present. Change daily and PRN.
  - hydrogel wafer or sheet if wound is painful. Secure with gauze wrap. Change every one to two days and PRN. *Note: Using a nonadherent dressing such as Telfa® and a topical silver product may result in a chemical reaction in which the cream will appear green when the dressing is removed.*
  - absorptive dressing and silver preparation if there is a high amount of drainage. Change daily and PRN.
- Secure nonadherent dressings with a bandage or gauze wrap, if possible. Avoid tape.
- Consider drawing an arrow on the secondary (cover, outer) dressing to reveal the direction of the skin tear. (The arrow should point in the opposite direction to that in which the skin flap was raised.) This will reduce the risk of further tissue damage when the dressing is removed. Date and initial the dressing, if this is your preference or facility policy.
- Complete an incident report, if this is your facility policy.
- Notify the healthcare provider and responsible party, according to facility policy.
- Document assessment and treatment findings and notifications.
- Review and update the care plan.
- Unless you are concerned that the wound may be contaminated, leave the dressing in place for five to seven days to promote healing. Contact the

healthcare provider promptly if signs or symptoms of infection are present. If potential contamination is suspected, inspect it daily for five days. If the wound has not healed in 14 days, assess for factors that may be preventing healing.

Australian recommendation

An Australian physician advocates the following procedure. The results have been promising, and we provide it as an alternative. However, do not use it without approval of your facility Quality Assessment and Assurance (QA&A) committee and proper healthcare provider's order.

Alternate (Australian) skin-tear procedure:

- Apply gentle pressure with a clean gauze sponge to stop bleeding. If unsuccessful, use an alginate dressing.
- Cleanse with normal saline or pH-neutral cleanser, according to facility policy.
- If there is major separation of the wound edges, approximate them with Steri-Strips.
- Apply a low-strength povidone iodine solution to the wound, leave in place for three minutes, then wash it off.
- Apply a small amount of hydrogel to the wound and cover with a foam dressing.
- Hold in place with a lightweight cohesive bandage. Leave the system in place for seven days, then remove the dressing, clean the wound, and replace the system.
- After the next seven days, remove the dressing and replace it with a patch of nonpreserved zinc paste bandage covered with foam and held in place with

a lightweight cohesive bandage. This will help strengthen the new skin. Leave in place for seven days. On removal, the wound should be healed; if not quite, repeat the zinc-paste-patch dressing system for another seven days.

Documentation

Document the following on occurrence, then weekly or according to facility policy until healed:

- Size
- Shape
- Location
- Stage or depth
- Bleeding or drainage
- First aid
- Notifications
- Treatment
- Dressing

Telephone orders

Document the following:

- Nursing assessment of the problem
- Healthcare provider, resident, and family notification and responses
- Order written and transcribed accurately and legibly:
    - Order read back and verified

  - Order noted
  - Checked any/all corresponding documents
  - Obtained documentation and diagnosis for new medication orders
  - PRN orders specify dosage, purpose, frequency, as indicated
  - Stop orders obtained, if indicated
- Treatment orders specify cleansing agent, treatment product, frequency, stop date (until healed)
- Orders transcribed to med, treatment, ADL sheets
- Meds/treatment products ordered from pharmacy:
  - Orders are accurate
  - Med/treatment/flow sheets prepared to reflect start and stop dates
- Completed/scheduled lab, x-ray, therapy, dietitian evaluation, AIMS test, etc.
- Care plan, nursing care instructions updated
- Communication sent to other departments, as indicated
- Consent/release form signed, if applicable

Note: If the resident experiences frequent or recurrent skin tears, list preventative measures on the care plan.

1. White, MW, Karam, S, and Cowell, B. 1994. Skin tears in frail elders: a practical approach to prevention. *Geriatric Nursing* 1994 Mar-Apr, 15(2):95–9.

Temperature, abnormalities related to temperature regulation

General information for any temperature abnormality

- Check vital signs:
    - Note whether hypo- or hypertension are present.
    - Medicate and recheck in four hours if temp > 101°F rectally or 100°F tympanic or orally. *Avoid the axillary method unless other methods cannot be used.*
- Note that the tympanic method of temperature is often not accurate because the thermometer is like a camera: It takes the temperature of whatever the lens is aimed at. The lens must be flat against the tympanic membrane, not tipped to the side:
    - To ensure an accurate reading, pull the ear up and back to straighten the ear canal. Insert the probe tip into the ear canal as far as it will go. Rotate the probe handle until it is aligned with the jaw, like speaking on the telephone. Quickly press the scan or activation button.
- Check for signs and symptoms of infection.
- Check for other signs and symptoms that are a clue to the cause of temperature abnormality, if unknown.
- Assess the presence or absence of chills.
- Assess the presence or absence of lethargy.
- Check for fingerstick blood glucose over 300.

- If the resident is on warfarin, monitor PT and INR, coagulation status; *monitor regularly for signs of bleeding if antibiotics/antiinflammatory drugs ordered.*
- Check for and consider recent laboratory values, if any.
- Check for and consider past history of fever of unknown origin (FUO), if any.
- Check for fecal impaction.
- Auscultate lungs and do a focused assessment of the respiratory system:
  - Determine whether there is a recent history of choking on food or fluid, even if incident was minor
- Monitor for signs/symptoms of dehydration and inadequate fluid intake:
  - Consider I&O monitoring
- Note any other changes from the resident's usual condition (i.e., what he or she is like on a normal day).
- Notify the healthcare provider of abnormal observations; *immediate* (emergency) notification is needed for a temperature *over 101°F* if sepsis is suspected for residents who are on dialysis or with diagnosed diseases of the immune system, such as HIV. Residents with other conditions needing immediate notification are those with the following:
  - Chemotherapy and radiation therapy
  - Leukemia
  - Lethargy
  - Chilling
  - Decreased fluid intake with or without signs of dehydration
  - Recent history of choking on food or fluid, even if minor

  - Abnormal lung sounds
  - Blood sugar over 300
- Routine reporting is necessary if the resident has a fever less than 101°F that has not responded to nursing measures within 12 hours.

Assess and document the following each shift:

Hypothermia

- Vital signs
- Changes in skin color
- Cyanosis of the lips or nail beds
- Sudden changes in temperature
- Marked changes in pulse, respirations, and blood pressure
- Respiratory distress
- Pain
- Changes in sensation
- Edema
- Shivering and chills
- Urinary output below 50 mL/hour
- Signs or symptoms of infection anywhere in body
- Condition of mucous membranes, signs and symptoms of dehydration (note that the area between the gums and cheek will stay moist even with a mouth breather *unless resident is dehydrated*)

Note: Observe the resident carefully. Shock, such as from a urinary tract infection, often results in hypothermia in elderly persons. This is an acute medical emergency.

Hyperthermia/hyperpyrexia

- Vital signs
- Temperature normal or slightly below or above
- Headache
- Weakness
- Fatigue
- Dizziness
- Loss of appetite
- Nausea and vomiting
- Muscle cramps in the arms, legs, or abdomen
- Pale skin color
- Rapid pulse and respirations
- Orthostatic hypotension
- Skin cool and moist
- Excessive perspiration
- Confusion
- Clumsiness, incoordination

The following are early signs and symptoms of heat stroke:

- Headache
- Dizziness
- Weakness
- Fatigue
- Skin hot and dry to touch

Unrecognized and untreated, the condition progressively worsens. Later signs and symptoms include the following:

- Extremely high fever
- Shortness of breath
- Slow, thready pulse or strong, rapid pulse
- Blood pressure may be low or difficult to hear/palpate
- Absence of perspiration
- Bizarre behavior
- Combativeness
- Seizures
- Loss of consciousness
- Lethargy, stupor, or coma
- Cardiac abnormalities
- Metabolic acidosis

- Respiratory alkalosis
- Severely low potassium levels
- Death

Tracheostomy

Assess and document the following each shift:

- Vital signs; note changes
- Capillary refill
- Initiate pulse oximetry if symptomatic
- Exhaustion, intolerance, or respiratory distress related to any procedure
- Changes in the resident's color
- Changes in the pulse oximeter or cardiac monitor
- Color and character of secretions (should be thin, white, or translucent; secretions are slightly sticky)

Report

- thick secretions
- yellow, green, brown, or red sputum
- red streaks in sputum

Transient ischemic attack (TIA)

Assess and document the following each shift:

- Vital signs
- Capillary refill
- Pulse oximetry
- Temporary lightheadedness/dizziness
- Variable changes in level of consciousness
- Confusion
- Speech disturbance
- Loss of vision
- Diplopia
- Numbness or weakness of one side of the face or an arm or leg
- Severe headache
- Mental confusion
- Difficulty speaking or understanding
- Impaired muscle coordination or impaired walking
- Paralysis on one side of the body
- Auscultation of the carotid artery (may reveal a bruit—an abnormal sound caused by blood flowing over the rough surface of one or both carotid arteries)

- Motor, sensory, and cognitive functions (during the ischemic period, these functions are temporarily affected)

Note: Symptoms are brief, often lasting less than an hour.

Unstable or postoperative resident observations

- Check for and consider recent laboratory values, if any
- Evaluate new medications and side effects, if any
- Monitor for signs/symptoms of dehydration and inadequate fluid intake (which causes hypovolemia):
  - Consider I&O monitoring

Assess and document the following one or more times each shift:

- Vital signs at specified frequency (usually no less often than every four hours)
- Capillary refill
- Pulse oximetry
- Decreased responsiveness or unresponsiveness
- Change in the level of responsiveness
- Increased restlessness accompanied by complaints of thirst
- Changes in blood pressure
- Weak, rapid, or irregular pulse
- Changes in temperature
- Changes in respiratory rate
- Difficulty breathing, labored or noisy respirations
- Nausea or vomiting

- Complaints of pain
- Increased drainage, wet or saturated dressings
- Active bleeding
- Coughing or choking

Urinary tract infection and genitourinary disorders

- Check for and consider recent laboratory values, if any
- Monitor for signs/symptoms of dehydration or inadequate fluid intake (which causes hypovolemia):
  - Consider I&O monitoring
- Note any other changes from the resident's usual condition (i.e., what he or she is like on a normal day)
- Determine whether the resident has a history of recurrent urinary tract infections (UTI) or has recently had a UTI
- Determine whether the resident has a catheter

Assess and document the following each shift:

- Vital signs
- Skin color and temperature
- Presence of fever, chills, vomiting, or abdominal rigidity
- Color, odor, and consistency of urine
- Presence or absence of sediment or mucus in urine
- Presence of hematuria
- Presence of abdominal distention

- Complaints of
  - suprapubic discomfort
  - bladder spasm
  - frequency, urgency, or hesitancy
  - burning or dysuria upon urination
- Presence or absence of nocturia
- Presence or absence of flank pain
- Voiding frequently in small amounts
- Lethargy
- Skin turgor (describe)
- Presence or absence of fluid retention, including edema, rales, periorbital edema; if lower-extremity edema present, measure with tape measure and record
- Evaluation or progress related to bowel and bladder management or retraining program, if any
- Presence of malaise (upper urinary tract)
- Presence of anorexia (upper urinary tract)
- Presence of nausea (upper urinary tract)
- I&O
- Presence or absence of penile or vaginal drainage
- Presence of constipation or impaction

- If resident is on warfarin, most recent PT and INR, coagulation status, and signs of internal bleeding (*monitor residents on warfarin every shift for signs of bleeding if antibiotics/antiinflammatory drugs ordered*)

Note: If resident has below normal temperature or is hypothermic, see "Sepsis."

Also see "Prerenal Azotemia and Acute Renal Failure."

UTI, signs and symptoms in cognitive impairment

Unfortunately, identifying signs and symptoms of UTI is often difficult in residents with communication problems and those who are cognitively impaired. This increases the risk of both over- and undertreatment. Symptoms of a UTI may be mild or absent. They are usually atypical. The resident may not mount a febrile response. In fact, the resident may become hypothermic or have a temperature below normal.[1,2] Because elderly persons may not mount a febrile response, fever may be defined as any increase over the upper limits of the resident's usual or normal daily temperature range. If infection is suspected, use the most accurate method available for taking the temperature. The rectal method is preferred. Avoid the axillary method unless no other alternatives exist. If a tympanic thermometer is used, make sure the technique is meticulous to prevent inaccurate readings. Signs and symptoms of infection vary widely, and an elderly resident usually presents differently than a younger adult.

Common, nonspecific symptoms of UTI include the following:

- Change in or abnormal vital signs
- Unexplained deterioration of physical function
- Change in mental status
- New or worsening cognitive impairment, increasing confusion

- Delirium
- Agitation, restlessness
- Lethargy
- Anorexia
- Decline in mobility
- Falls
- Nonspecific complaints of feeling ill
- New episode of incontinence, increased frequency of incontinence, or nocturia
- Cough
- Nausea, vomiting
- Abdominal pain
- Change in appearance, color, or odor of urine that does not promptly respond to increased fluids
- Body language or other behavior suggesting pain

These signs and symptoms suggest sepsis, regardless of whether the resident is febrile. Monitor the resident carefully for and notify the healthcare provider promptly about any of the following:

- Hypotension
- Tachycardia
- Hypothermia
- Dyspnea, respiratory distress

For a diagnosis of UTI, a resident *without an indwelling catheter* typically meets three or more of these criteria:

- Fever (> 38°C) or chills
- New or increased burning pain on urination
- New flank or suprapubic pain or tenderness
- Changes in character of urine and worsening mental function

For a diagnosis of UTI, a resident *with an indwelling catheter* typically meets two or more of these criteria:

- Fever (> 38°C) or chills
- New flank or suprapubic pain or tenderness
- Changes in character of urine
- Worsening mental function

1. Gomolin, I, Kathpalia, R, and Sangwan, A. 2002. UTI in long-term care and nursing home patients. *Current Treatment Options in Infectious Diseases* 2002, 4:7–13.

2. Orenstein, R, and Wong, ES. 1999. Urinary tract infections in adults. *Am Fam Physician* 1999; 59:1225–1234.

Weight loss, cachexia, malnutrition

Assess and document the following at the frequency specified by facility protocol. Consider at least one complete assessment of the resident's nutrition status weekly:

- Vital signs
- Daily or weekly weight, as ordered or per protocol
- Whether the resident needs help eating and drinking
- I&O, if fluid consumption is also a problem
- Whether the resident consumes less than 50% of meals and snacks (document special approaches, such as six small meals a day, and resident response)
- Mouth pain, dental problems, or missing teeth
- Difficulty chewing or swallowing (may need evaluation for modified texture food)
- Coughs or chokes while eating, swallows many times with each mouthful
- Dull, dry hair or hair falling out at an abnormal rate
- Red, swollen lips (may have fissures at corners)
- Red, swollen gums
- Dry mouth with fissures of mucous membranes/tongue (note that the area between the gums and cheek will stay moist even with a mouth breather *unless resident is dehydrated*)
- Red or purple, inflamed tongue, smooth in appearance

- Pale color, dry skin, sunken cheeks
- Fragile nails (may be spoon shaped)
- Diarrhea, anorexia
- Weakness, muscle wasting, peripheral neuropathy
- Loss of muscle mass
- Slow wound healing; ecchymosis; dry, flaky skin; may have edema as a result of low protein
- Listlessness
- Personality and behavior changes
- Fatigue, progressing to complete exhaustion
- Depression, crying spells, withdrawal
- Apathy, lack of initiative
- Skin condition, increased risk of pressure ulcers
- Accidents and incidents, increased risk of falls
- Abnormal laboratory values, particularly albumin, total protein, cholesterol, hemoglobin, and hematocrit; possible abnormal magnesium and potassium
- Diabetes, chronic obstructive pulmonary disease, cancer, HIV, Parkinson's disease, Huntington's disease, and other chronic diseases
- Death

If a resident begins losing weight, assess, document, request dietitian evaluation, initiate I&O and calorie-count monitoring, and take appropriate nursing action (including notifications):

- Vital signs
- Evaluate overall status of hydration (weight loss and dehydration often go hand in hand)
- Weight loss over the past six months
- Type of diet
- Resident's ability to feed self:
  - If resident feeds self, evaluate ability to see the food
  - If resident has had CVA, consider hemianopsia (blindness in visual field); if he or she is leaving food on one side of the plate, turn the plate to see whether this makes a difference and document your findings.
- Dental problems interfering with ability to eat
- Shortness of breath interfering with ability to eat
- Distractions, noise, or other environmental problems interfering with ability to eat
- Swallowing problems (*note:* also see "Dysphagia")
- Wandering interfering with ability to eat
- Improper positioning (leaning, table too far away, table too high) interfering with ability to eat
- Factors, such as tremors, interfering with the resident's ability to bring the food to the mouth
- Feeding assistance available and given
- Cognitive loss

- Wandering and other behavioral problems increasing the resident's caloric needs
- Medical diagnoses, such as Huntington's disease, cancer, infection, or pressure ulcer increasing the resident's caloric needs
- Depression
- Medications affecting appetite; drugs that suppress the appetite but may not be considered are as follows:
  - Aldactone
  - Antacids
  - Anticonvulsants
  - Antipsychotics
  - Aspirin
  - B-adrenergic antagonists
  - Barbiturates
  - Benzodiazepines
  - Bumex
  - Capoten
  - Carbidopa
  - Clonidine
  - Digitoxin
  - Digoxin
  - Dyazide

- Flagyl
- H_2 blockers
- Haldol
- Iron
- Levodopa
- Nonsteroidal antiinflammatory drugs (NSAIDs)
- Prozac
- Theophylline

Evaluate

- the accuracy of recorded food intake.
- the accuracy of recorded supplement intake.
- the need for supplement at med pass.
- recent laboratory values, if any.
- new medications and side effects, if any.
- the adequacy of fluid intake compared with body needs.
- any signs/symptoms of dehydration or inadequate fluid intake (which causes hypovolemia):
    - Consider I&O monitoring
- the accuracy of recorded quantity of tube feeding and any need for increased calories.
- the tube-feeding formula—is resident receiving a half-strength or three-quarter-strength tube-feeding formula? If so, he or she is receiving only half

or three-fourth's the amount of calories, as well (estimate calories in tube feeding; 1 mL = one calorie).

- check skin for presence of new pressure ulcers.
- serum cholesterol; other labs.

Weight-loss nursing assessment

- Check vital signs.
- Assess and document the following in nursing notes:
  - Resident's eating abilities
  - Whether specific mealtime assistance is required
  - Choking/swallowing problems, risk factors for choking, need for speech evaluation for swallowing/choking
  - Refusals of food and fluids
  - Normal meal consumption
- Evaluate I&O, if on record; if not, initiate I&O monitoring.
- Determine whether visual impairment inhibiting the resident's ability to eat; also consider visual impairment (hemianopsia) related to CVA and request evaluation if necessary.
- Consider condition of teeth and mouth and whether it interferes with ability to eat; request dental evaluation, if necessary.
- Consider whether depression is a contributing factor; if so, request social services consult.
- Evaluate medications for their effect on eating ability; request pharmacist evaluation at next regular visit.

- Establish and initiate a plan of care to reverse as many risk factors as possible.
- Ask the dietary manager to evaluate likes; dislikes; cultural, religious, ethnic, and other food preferences.
- Consider the dietitian's recommendations already on the chart:
  - *Note:* Dietitian calculations for daily caloric and fluid intake on care plan, I&O sheet, and meal intake sheet
- Consider fluid intake with a trial of I&O monitoring; residents who are not eating often do not consume sufficient fluids.
- Develop a total nutritional plan of care that addresses the resident's individual risk factors and unique individual needs. Communicate the plan to the nursing assistant staff, and others who serve meals or feed the resident. The plan should address maintenance of the resident's existing abilities.

Weight loss, new healthcare provider orders

- Check vital signs.
- Notify healthcare provider, resident, family:
  - Document response
- Request order for nutritional med pass (two Cal HN with each med pass).
- Schedule daily or weekly weight, as ordered or per protocol.
- Notify dietary manager.
- Request dietitian consultation.
- Initiate I&O monitoring; evaluate for adequacy based on dietitian calculations after three days. If fluid intake does not meet or exceed dietitian recommendation, continue I&O monitoring.

- Initiate a three-day calorie count pending dietitian visit.
- Charge nurse should evaluate and document all meal consumption.
- Flag chart for review during next care conference.
- Update care plan, nursing care instructions; do an interim update to reflect new orders above.

Section III:

Enteral and parenteral nutrition

Total parenteral nutrition

Assess and document the following each shift:

- Check vital signs
- Describe quality, character, and rate of pulse
- Monitor for
  - hypotension
  - fever, which may indicate acute infection; describe nursing interventions
  - chills and shaking (signs of acute infection)
- Assess lung sounds
- Describe presence or absence of
  - dyspnea
  - cyanosis
- Describe appearance of insertion site: check for pain, redness, edema, warmth, drainage, and leakage
- Monitor intake and output
- Order fingerstick blood sugar at specified frequency
- Monitor for signs of
  - hypoglycemia: tachycardia, diaphoresis, headache, irritability, restlessness, lethargy, and blood glucose below 70

  - hyperglycemia: elevated blood sugar, increased thirst, lethargy, visual disturbances

- Weigh daily
- Monitor for signs of
  - fluid overload: sacral or pedal edema, weight gain, increased blood pressure, and bounding pulse
  - fluid deficit: poor skin turgor, sunken eyeballs, dry mucous membranes, tachycardia, hypotension, and weight loss
- Note complaints of abdominal pain or back pain
- Monitor for rash or urticaria; describe
- Assess sterile technique used for dressing changes and accessing the central line
- Assess I&O

Tube feeding

Tube feeding orders specify product, calories, method of administration, amount of feeding or continuous drip/pump rate:

- Half- and three-quarter-strength formulas should always have a three- to five-day stop date, or an order to progressively increase the formula to full strength (remember: half-strength formula = half the calories needed each day!).
- Always initiate I&O monitoring when obtaining a tube-feeding order; documenting the total ordered amount of fluids on a flow sheet each day is not sufficient. The amount will vary, depending on flushes and medications given.
- For continuous feeding, question the physician about whether the daily caloric allotment may be given over 23 hours instead of 24. Write the order to turn off pump/continuous feeding an hour a day for bathing, therapy, etc.

  A continuous order should be written as follows:

  Formula type _________ at _________ mL _____ hour
  via ❑ gravity ❑ pump ❑ bolus. Total calories per 24 hours is ___________.

  The water flush orders should read as follows:

  Flush tube with __________mL water or _________ (minimum 30 mL–50 mL) before and after *each* medication is given and each time feeding is stopped or started. (Avoid crushed meds, if possible; obtain orders for liquid meds when available.) Flush tube with _________ mL free water every ________ hours to total __________ mL in 24 hours.

Tube feeding

- Document at least one residual check per shift; feeding returned to stomach. (If a resident is receiving continuous feeding, stop the feeding 15 minutes before checking for stomach residual.) Note HOB elevated 30° to 45° during residual checks. Facility policies or physician orders should specify when to stop feeding and notify physician. (The feeding is withheld if the amount withdrawn exceeds 100 mL or one and a half times the amount delivered in one hour by continuous administration.)
- Specify the procedure (e.g., checking pH, air injection, and auscultation; measuring length of tube, etc.) and frequency for placement checks and residual checks; document whether placement was checked prior to each medication and feeding via _____ method.
- Clarify with the physician what action to take if tube plugs and changes become necessary.
- Tube orders and care plan should specify that head of bed be elevated at least 30° to 45° when feeding is being given and for one hour after. (Care plan should also reflect increased risk to skin related to HOB elevation.)
- Notify the dietary manager about the order and request a dietitian consult.
- Update care plan and nursing care instructions
- The following information may be documented on a flow sheet related to tube-feeding care every shift:
  - Oral and nasal (mucous membrane) care (specify frequency)
  - Care needed for healing or infected stoma, if applicable
  - pump is free from dust, dirt, and residue every shift; damp-dusted once each day

- Visual check of resident position and tube placement every _____ hour (s)
- Change feeding bag and tubing every 24 hours (unless a closed ready-to-hang formula is used)
- Head of bed elevated 30° or more (specify when, if intermittent)

Venipuncture and IV therapy

- Check vital signs.
- Never chart IVs in advance.
- Initial the IV record immediately after starting the IV.
- Document other care (e.g., changing dressings or tubing) on the correct form.
- If the resident is not on I&O, place an I&O work sheet at the bedside and inform the nursing assistants and other staff that I&O has been initiated.
- Document your nursing or systemic assessment immediately before the IV was started. Include vital signs, such as pulse or blood pressure, and other monitoring as warranted by resident condition, physician orders, and facility policies.
- The physician's order should specify:
  - Infusion route
  - Type of access device
  - Type of base solution
  - Specific medication and additives
  - Rate of infusion
  - Dosage
  - Frequency of administration

IV orders should be written as follows:

1,000 mL ______________ every __________ via ❑ gravity ❑ pump

At a minimum, nursing documentation for IV start should list the following:

- Size and type of device used
- Date and time of start and finish of infusion. Also label time on bag.
- Type of solution
- Type of additives
- Resident assessment—blood pressure, pulse, etc.
- Site accessed
- Complications, resident response, interventions
- Condition of the site upon IV discontinuation

Start IV: _____ gauge __________ (longdwell, butterfly, etc.) started in _________________ vein (figure 3.1). Specify cephalic, ulnar, median antebrachial, intermediate cephalic or cubital, basilic, etc. (The median and cephalic veins are the safest choice.) using aseptic technique on _________ (first or second) attempt and flow of solution is established.

Figure 3.1

The median and cephalic veins are usually the best choice for an IV because they are large, relatively straight, and less likely to infiltrate. They also permit the resident limited mobility without fear of infiltration.

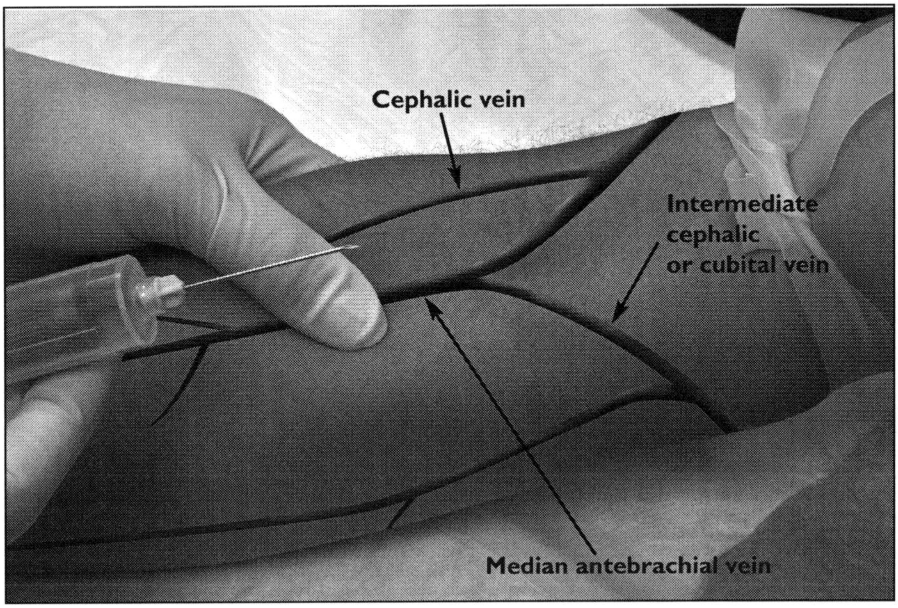

Marking the container

Your facility will have policies regarding information to mark on the IV container, or the pharmacy may provide a label with some or all of this information. Use a label. Never write on a plastic bottle or bag with ink or permanent marker. The IV bag or bottle should list the following:

- Resident's name
- Room number
- Date and time

- Container number
- Flow rate ordered
- Duration of the infusion
- Your name or initials
- Add a time tape, if used by your facility

Assess for and document each shift (documentation may be managed on a flow sheet):

Potential complications of IV therapy

- Bleeding from the venipuncture site
- Ecchymosis
- Hematoma, a larger collection of blood under the skin
- Air embolus—signs and symptoms include respiratory distress; cyanosis; weak, rapid pulse; decreased blood pressure; loss of consciousness; and cardiac arrest
- Fluid overload—signs and symptoms include respiratory distress and cardiac arrest—early signs and symptoms are rapid respirations, shortness of breath, rapid pulse, increased blood pressure, and distended neck veins
- Phlebitis and localized infection—signs and symptoms include redness, swelling, or a red streak at the needle insertion site, and drainage from the venipuncture site:
  - After initiating IV therapy, if the resident develops a phlebitis, remove the catheter and assess the degree of phlebitis according to Intravenous Nursing Standards of Practice:

1+: pain, erythema or edema, no streaking, palpable cord

2+: pain, erythema or edema, streak formation, no palpable cord

3+: pain, erythema or edema, streak formation, palpable cord

- Generalized infection—signs and symptoms include malaise, fever, and chills

Signs and symptoms of infiltration

- Pain/burning at the insertion site
- Swelling at the insertion site
- Skin cool to touch; may be lighter in color at the insertion site
- Rigid, taut skin near the insertion site
- Infusion rate has slowed or stopped
- Dressing covering the insertion site is damp or wet
- No backflow of blood into IV tubing when the bag is lowered below the insertion site

IV troubleshooting and nursing action

Problem: IV stops dripping

- Confirm that fluid is present in the infusion container
- Check for kinks or obstructions in tubing
- Make sure all roller clamps and slide clamps are open
- Check for signs and symptoms of infiltration
- Lower the bag or bottle below heart level and check the tubing for blood return

- Make sure the IV pole and height of the bag is 30 to 40 inches above the insertion site
- Reposition the resident to see whether this affects the flow of solution
- Continue to monitor the infusion frequently

Problem: Flow rate is too slow

- Check for signs and symptoms of infiltration.
- Reposition the resident to see whether this affects the flow of solution.
- Check for kinks or obstructions in tubing.
- Make sure all roller clamps and slide clamps are open.
- Make sure the IV pole and height of the bag is 30 to 40 inches above the insertion site; try raising the pole to see whether this affects the flow rate.
- Reposition the catheter at the hub. Elevate the hub slightly. Place one or more sterile 2 x 2 gauze pads under the hub and redress the site.
- As a last resort, disconnect the tubing from the hub. If the fluid flows freely through the tubing, the problem is with the catheter. Discontinue it and restart the IV in another location.
- Continue to monitor the infusion frequently.

Problem: Flow rate is too fast

- Adjust the roller clamp to slow the rate
- Time it to make sure it is accurate, as ordered by the physician

Problem: Flow rate alternates between slow and fast

- Reposition the resident's arm.
- Monitor the flow rate for a few minutes.
- Apply an arm board, if necessary (remember: the arm board is probably considered a restraint).
- Remove the dressing and reposition the catheter at the hub. Place a sterile gauze pad under the hub and redress the site.
- Continue to monitor the infusion frequently.

Section IV:

Observations and relevant documentation of ADLs

Observations of ADLs

Activity	Observations
Activities of daily living	• What the resident can do independently • The resident's need for assistance, how much assistance, and type of assistance needed • The resident's ability to tolerate activity (e.g., does he or she become fatigued, short of breath, etc.) • The resident's motivation, preferences, and abilities
Bathing	• Does not resist bathing • Ability for unassisted self-bathing • Ability for self-bathing with an adaptive device; describe device • Needs partial assistance with bathing • Needs total assistance with bathing
Dressing and grooming	• Overall appearance—tidy, untidy, neat, clean. • Ability for unassisted self-dressing. • Ability for self-dressing with an adaptive device. • Needs partial assistance with dressing. • Needs total assistance with dressing.

Activity	Observations
Dressing and grooming *(cont.)*	• Requires frequent, but not constant, one-to-one, hands-on assistance for grooming or the retrieval and arrangement of clothing. This includes assistance with prostheses. • Requires continuous, one-to-one assistance and supervision during the entire activity. If the staff person is not present to guide, teach, motivate, or provide hands-on care, he or she will not complete the activity. • The recipient does not participate in the dressing/grooming process.
Transfers	• Independent; no assistance required, but may use equipment such as railings, trapeze, etc. • Requires PRN assistance for transfers. • One to transfer: Continuously requires one person for physical or verbal assist on 60% or more of the transfers. Specify when assistance is required and for what reason. • Two to transfer: Requires assistance of two or more during the entire activity on 60% or more of the transfers. Specify when assistance is required and for what reason. • Not transferred: May be transferred to a stretcher or chair once a week or less, excluding transfers to bath or toilet. • Describe other devices (e.g., mechanical lift).

Activity	Observations
Walking	• Difficulty getting up and down • Needs an assistive device, such as a cane or walker • Safety awareness • Gait steady, unsteady, shuffling, rigid, etc. • Posture • Sudden onset of falls, difficulty balancing • Walks unassisted; requires device, such as cane, crutch, or walker • Requires assistance for uneven surfaces or difficult ambulation, such as stairs or ramps • Uses wheelchair and may require physical assistance for difficult maneuvers, such as elevators or ramps or longer distances; may be able to walk, but generally does not
Position, movement	• Ability to position/reposition self • Need for staff to reposition • Special positioning aids • Ability to move unassisted • Presence of contractures • Able/unable to move • Movements shaky, jerking, tremors, muscle spasms, etc. • Presence or absence of pain upon movement • Deformity, edema

Activity	Observations
Position, movement *(cont.)*	• Normal or abnormal range of motion • Ability to sit, stand, move • Independent bed mobility, transfers, ambulation • Paralysis in one or more extremities (hemiplegia, paraplegia, tetraplegia [quadriplegia], diplegia, etc.)
Contractures	• None • One extremity (limb) affected • Two extremities (limbs) affected • Three extremities (limbs) affected • Four extremities (limbs) affected • Fetal position • Note degree/stage of contracture • Note measures to prevent additional contractures
Eating	• Food likes and dislikes, refusals. • Feeding ability, need for assistance, how much assistance, type of assistance needed. • Requires adaptive device(s) for independent eating. • Able to eat finger foods only without assistance; requires assistance with utensils. • Percentage of meal consumed. • Difficulty chewing or swallowing; coughing, choking. • Distracted or wanders at meals, needs to be refocused.

Activity	Observations
Eating *(cont.)*	• Independent or does not receive nutrition (e.g., advance directive). • Intermittent assistance: Requires verbal or physical assistance less than 60% of the time. • In a restorative feeding program, an assessment of the resident's potential should be documented. The restorative program should be provided for at least two meals per day. Verbal cuing must be specific and related to plan of care. • Requires assistance to syringe or spoon feed 60% or more of the time. Specify when assistance is required, the type of assistance provided, and for what reason. • Receives nonoral feedings for 60% or more of his or her nutrition using a tube such as an NG, G, or PEG tube, or administration of TPN via a central line. Document the frequency, amounts, routes, and times at which the nonoral feedings were administered.
Drinking	• Ability to take a drink at will without assistance • Ability to drink from straw, cup; or need for special device • Need for assistance, how much assistance, type of assistance needed. • Beverage preferences • Accepts or refuses water, if offered • Fluid intake • Difficulty swallowing liquids; coughing, choking • Requires I&O monitoring

Activity	Observations
Toileting	• Independent, may require special equipment. Performs his or her own incontinent care, self-catheterization, ostomy care, etc. • Requires assistance but can be left alone for privacy. Assistance may include transferring on and off the commode, cleansing after elimination, adjusting clothing, or washing hands. • Requires physical or verbal assist or supervision during entire toileting process, excluding incontinent care, and cannot be left alone. Document the functional, medical, or behavioral reason the resident cannot be left alone. • Incontinent or has an indwelling catheter. Includes staff-administered ostomy care, incontinence care using protective padding, incontinence briefs, changing clothes, or a propped urinal. Document and describe the type of assistance staff provide 60% or more of the time. • Taken to the toilet by staff every two hours during waking hours, or more often if needed, as incontinence management. Stays dry 60% or more of the time as the result of being toileted by staff. Residents who receive in-and-out catheterization by the staff two or more times each day are included in this category. Document and describe the type of assistance staff provide 60% or more of the time.
Urinary elimination	• Frequency of elimination. • Inability to urinate, or voiding frequently in small amounts. • Will the resident use the bathroom if given the opportunity? • Color, clarity, odor, amount of urine. • Presence of mucus, sediment, or other abnormalities in urine.

Activity	Observations
Urinary elimination *(cont.)*	• Pain, burning, frequency of urination. • Does the resident have a urinary catheter; if so, is it draining properly, leaking, etc.? • Continent. • Incontinent three times a day or less. Includes residents who receive assistance in control of dribbling. • Incontinent only at night. • Incontinent four or more times in a 24-hour period. Includes residents with external catheters, urostomies, and ileal conduits. • Requires indwelling catheter or intermittent catheterization. • Requires I&O monitoring.
Bowel elimination	• Frequency of elimination. • Will the resident use the bathroom if given the opportunity? • Is the resident incontinent? • Appearance of stool: presence of blood, mucus, parasites, or foreign matter, liquid or solid stool. • Abnormal color to stool (black, clay color, etc.). • Small or extremely large stool. • Loose, watery stool. • Complaints of pain, constipation, diarrhea, or bleeding. • Excessive gas (flatus). • Requires monitoring for tendency toward constipation, fecal impaction.

Activity	Observations
Bowel elimination *(cont.)*	• Continent. • Has an ostomy and is independent with its care. • Resident is incontinent one to three times per week. • Incontinent four or more times per week. • Requires assistance with an ileostomy or colostomy; includes nursing care or teaching self-care.
Vision and hearing	• Vision is adequate in most situations. Able to see in good light (with corrective lenses, if customarily worn). • Visually impaired; however, supervision or physical assistance is not needed for visually cued tasks. • Visually impaired, and supervision or physical assistance is required to complete visually cued tasks. • Cannot determine visual acuity. • Hears speech at regular conversational levels even in noise and in groups. • Hears speech at regular conversational levels but may have difficulty hearing in other than quiet listening conditions or in one-on-one situations. • Hears speech only when lip-reading and relies on other cues. Can hear most conversation only when the speaker's face is clearly visible. • Hears only some speech sounds even when lip-reading and using other cues. Misses most conversation, even when the speaker's face is clearly visible. • Hearing cannot be used for communication.

Activity	Observations
Vision and hearing *(cont.)*	• Uses an adaptive, assistive, or electronic device or special computer software for communication. • Cannot determine hearing.
Functional communication *(the process of making one's needs known—includes verbal and nonverbal communication, but does not include language barriers)*	• Communicates without difficulty. • Communicates, but requires extra time or assistance. • Communicates only basic needs. • Communicates occasionally, but communication is nonfunctional for expression of basic needs. Resident may require frequent repetition or simplification of spoken instructions. • Does not communicate needs. • Cannot determine.
Level of consciousness	• Conscious—responsive; may be listless or lethargic, but is aware of surroundings • Semiconscious—unaware of surroundings, but reacts to sensory stimuli • Comatose—persistent unconsciousness and unresponsiveness from which the resident cannot be aroused • Persistent vegetative state • Change in consciousness, awareness, or alertness • Ability to respond verbally or nonverbally • Responds to spoken word • Responds to touch • Responds to pain only • Sleepy for no apparent reason

Activity	Observations
Orientation, memory, mental clarity	• Requires intervention less than once per week. Capable of functioning independently in his or her environment. Can be occasionally forgetful. • Requires intervention one to six days per week. • Requires daily intervention from staff, including assistance for ADLs, due to the documented orientation problem. Document and describe the orientation problem, required staff intervention, and frequency of intervention. *Use of the term "reality orientation" is not a sufficient description.* • Complete disorientation or incoherence. Document and describe the orientation problem, required staff intervention, and frequency of intervention. *Use of the term "reality orientation" is not a sufficient description.* • Undetermined. Does not include residents who speak another language or are nonverbal.
Behavior *(disruptive behaviors cause the staff to immediately stop or change what they are doing to control a situation; although some nondisruptive behaviors may be irritating, they do not create a need for immediate staff intervention)*	• No behavior problems reported or exhibited. • Requires immediate staff intervention one to four days per month, but not weekly. • Requires immediate staff intervention one to six days per week. • Requires staff intervention once a day or more. • Resident is verbally aggressive or uses abusive language (e.g., swearing, threatening, baiting/provoking, or yelling). Document and describe behavior, staff response, and frequency.

Activity	Observations
Behavior *(cont.)*	• Resident is physically aggressive, combative, or assaultive to self or others (e.g., hitting self or others, throwing objects at others). Document and describe behavior, staff response, and frequency. • Other disruptive acts, such as inappropriate undressing, stealing, smearing feces, destruction of property, wandering, sexually displaying themselves, or refusing treatment. (Do not include nonphysical behavior such as withdrawal, paranoia, etc.) Document and describe behavior, staff response, and frequency.
Restraints/safety devices	• Not used • Occasional use only (less than once a week) • Days/evenings only • Nights only • Days/evenings and nights • Geriatric chair • Vest/belt • Wrist/mitten • Side rails
Sleeping	• Ability to sleep, or can't sleep • Sleeps constantly • Awake at night • Sleeps during day

Activity	Observations
Sleeping *(cont.)*	• Awakens easily • Difficult to awaken • Moves about in sleep • Needs to be awakened for toileting • Repositions self or needs to be repositioned by staff
Unstable or special health problems	• Resident is being actively monitored or treated for one or more unstable, symptomatic health problems, such as acute exacerbation of a chronic illness, frequent seizures, internal bleeding, acute infection, dyspnea, edema, tremors, pressure ulcers, surgical incisions, etc. Hemiplegia, paraplegia, and tetraplegia (quadriplegia) fall into this category. Document the functional, medical, or behavioral problem; frequency of monitoring or assistance; and specific staff responses or interventions. • Recent fracture. • Recent amputation. • Stage III or IV pressure ulcer(s). • Oxygen administration. • Respiratory therapy. • Cancer radiation or chemotherapy. • Blood transfusion(s). • Renal dialysis, including both hemodialysis and peritoneal dialysis in the facility or at an outside clinic. • Oral/nasal suctioning daily or more often.

Activity	Observations
Unstable or special health problems *(cont.)*	• Oral/nasal suctioning one or two times a week. • Oral/nasal suctioning three to five times a week. • Tracheostomy care daily or more often. • Tracheostomy care one or two times a week. • Tracheostomy care three to five times a week. • Ventilator/respirator: Describe and state service provided and frequency of use. • Wound dressings daily or more often. • Wound dressings one or two times a week. • Wound dressings three to five times a week. • Receiving hospice services or terminal care. Document condition and prognosis (such as 6 months or less).
Therapy, ADL, bowel and bladder, or restorative nursing program(s)	• State type of service(s) provided. • State frequency and duration. • Identify goals. • State reason service is being given.

For additional documentation information and task analyses for ADLs and declines, go to *www.kfmc.org/providers/Nursing_Homes/nhproviders.adl.html.*

Section V:

Useful assessment tools

ABCD scale

The ABCD score is being used to successfully predict the risk of having a stroke in persons who have previously experienced a TIA. The tool is simple to score and is based on a resident's age, blood pressure, clinical features, and duration of symptoms. The ABCD score can be used to estimate the risk of a full-blown stroke in the seven days after a TIA.

Predicting strokes

Factor	**Score**
Age over 60	1
Elevated blood pressure	1
Symptoms: - Weakness on one side of body - Speech difficulty	2
Symptoms: - Weakness on one side of body (only)	1
Symptoms: - Neither	0
Duration of symptoms: - More than 60 minutes	2
Duration of symptoms - 10–59 minutes	1
Duration of symptoms: - Less than 10 minutes	0
Total score	

An ABCD score of 5 is a strong predictor of impending stroke. A score of 6 necessitates not only emergency investigation and treatment but also admission to hospital during the acute phase, researchers note. Even if a stroke can't be prevented, being in the hospital should allow for immediate clot-clearing if one occurs.

Source: Lancet, *online June 21, 2005.*

Admission assessment, complete physical assessment

- Vital signs
- Respirations:
  - Normal breathing is effortless, quiet, and regular
- Breathing patterns:
  - Eupnea
  - Cheyne-Stokes
  - Cluster breathing
  - Hyperventilation
- Pulses:
  - Peripheral: Identify pulse rhythm, volume, and rate
  - Apical: Listen with the diaphragm of stethoscope
- Locate apex of heart, usually at the left 5th intercostal at the midclavicular line:
  - Note strength and regularity of rhythm
  - Count rate (count one full minute if the rhythm is irregular)
- Blood pressure
- Any signs of distress indicating a problem, potential worsening, or emergency
- Level of consciousness:
  - Speech

  - Orientation
- Eyes:
  - Pupil size, response to light
  - Extraocular eye movements
  - Accommodation
- Mouth:
  - Skin color around lips and tip of nose (checking for circumoral cyanosis)
  - Mucous membranes for moisture (area between gums and cheek will stay moist even with a mouth breather *unless resident is dehydrated*)
- Neck:
  - Neck vein distention
- Anterior chest
- Heart sounds (listen with the diaphragm of stethoscope)
- Breath sounds:
  - Vesicular: Low, breezy, soft sounds heard over the periphery of the lung fields
  - Bronchovesicular: Equal inspiration and expiration, medium quality, heard over the mainstem bronchi
  - Bronchial: Course, loud sound heard over the trachea
- Abdomen:
  - Observe the abdomen for symmetry, contour, movement
  - Listen in each of the four quadrants for bowel sounds

- Lightly palpate; check for tenderness, bladder distention

- Upper extremities, CMS checks:
  - Circulation: Capillary refill, radial pulses
  - Motion/sensation
  - Hand grasps
  - Push/pull
  - Straight arm raise
- Lower extremities, CMS checks:
  - Circulation: Capillary refill, posterior tibial and dorsalis pedis pulses
  - Motion/sensation
  - Push/pull
  - Leg raise
- Posterior chest:
  - Listen to breath sounds; while listening to either the anterior or posterior chest, be sure to auscultate the right middle lobe
- Paralysis and related definitions: Remember that paralysis affects more than the ability to move part of the body. True paralysis affects voluntary movement, strength, and sensation. Paralysis is defined as a complete loss of strength in an affected limb or muscle group. (Paralysis may affect a single muscle, but it typically affects one entire region of the body. A pattern or distribution of weakness is a clue or key to identifying the origin or location of the nerve damage that is causing the paralysis).

- *Diplegia*-paralysis of the same region on both sides of the body, such as both hands or arms.
- *Hemiparesis*-weakness on one side of the body, such as the left side of the face, left arm, or left leg.
- *Hemiplegia*-paralysis on one side of the body, such as the left side of the face, left arm, or left leg.
- *Monoplegia*-paralysis of one limb.
- *Paraplegia*-paralysis of the trunk; usually below the waist, including both legs and both feet.
- *Quadrilpegia*-see tetraplegia (In 1991, The American Spinal Cord Association published the recommendation to change the terminology used in the US to concur with the rest of the world. The Association recommends that the term "tetraplegia" be used instead of "quadriplegia").
- *Tetraplegia*-paralysis of the trunk, most commonly below the neck; commonly both arms and both legs, but some residents have limited shoulder or arm movement depending on the site of injury.

Assessing for bruits

A *bruit* in the carotid artery is an indication of cardiovascular disease. When auscultated with a stethoscope, it makes a sound similar to a "swishing." Any large blood vessel can be auscultated for a bruit. To assess the carotid artery for a bruit,

1. Gently locate the artery on one side of the neck.
2. Palpate the artery. Determine whether a thrill, or slight vibration is present.
3. Place the stethoscope over the carotid artery, beginning at the jaw line.
4. Ask the resident to hold his or her breath.
5. Lightly press the diaphragm. Auscultate while moving down the length of the artery to the clavicle.
6. Repeat on the other side.
7. Note that if you feel vibration or hear a swishing sound, this suggests vessel narrowing.
8. Inform the physician of your findings and take other appropriate nursing action.
9. Document your findings.

Cincinnati Pre-Hospital Stroke Scale, The

The Cincinnati Pre-Hospital Stroke Scale is a sensitive, quick examination for stroke. This assessment can readily be used by long-term care nursing personnel. Early identification of cerebrovascular accident (CVA) and transient ischemic attack (TIA) in the long-term care facility can have a dramatic effect of the mortality and morbidity of the residents. Using the Cincinnati Pre-Hospital Stroke Scale will help you to quickly and accurately identify the neurological status of a resident presenting with CVA/TIA signs and symptoms. Various studies have validated the accuracy of this assessment in the prehospital setting. In one study, people with one of these three findings—as a new event—had a 72% probability of an ischemic stroke. If all three findings were present, the probability of an acute stroke is estimated to be more than 85%.

Thrombolytic ("clot buster") drugs must be administered at an acute care hospital within three hours of onset of symptoms for effective results. The hospital must first take time to evaluate the resident and conduct diagnostic tests. Take stroke monitoring seriously and monitor the time frame carefully. These guidelines will help identify residents who will benefit from drug therapy. Keep the physician apprised of your findings. Careful assessment is essential. Remember, signs of stroke can be very subtle. Rapidly recognizing signs and symptoms, assessing the resident, and arranging for rapid emergency ambulance transport are the keys to helping the resident.

The Cincinnati test

The Cincinnati test consists of three parts: arm drift, facial droop, and speech impairment.

Arm drift

Ask the resident to extend his or her arms, palms up. If he or she has had a stroke, the neurological deficit will cause the affected hand to roll over, then drift downward. Take the following steps:

- Have the resident close his or her eyes and hold both arms out:
  - Normal: Both arms move the same way, or both arms do not move at all
  - Abnormal: One arm does not move or one arm drifts down compared with the other arm
- Other findings, such as hand grip, may be helpful

Facial droop

Observe the resident's face while it is relaxed. Look at the normal contours and creases. Next, ask the resident to smile as if to show the upper teeth. The face may appear normal in a relaxed position but asymmetrical when the resident smiles. An asymmetrical appearance suggests a stroke. Take the following steps:

- Have the resident show his or her teeth or smile:
  - Normal: Both sides of the face move equally well
  - Abnormal: One side of the face does not move as well as the other side, or does not move at all

Speech impairment

Stand where the resident can see your face. Ask him or her to repeat a simple phrase, such as "You can't teach an old dog new tricks." If the resident cannot repeat the entire phrase, suspect a stroke.

- Have the resident say, "You can't teach an old dog new tricks":
    - Normal: Resident uses correct words with no slurring
    - Abnormal: Resident slurs words, uses inappropriate words, or is unable to speak

Glasgow Coma Scale

The Glasgow Coma Scale is used to monitor neurologic dysfunction after trauma, stroke, and other neurological illnesses and injuries. The nurse determines the best response the resident can make to stimuli. Higher point values are assigned to responses that indicate increased awareness and arousal. The tool is simple, but effective. It is an excellent, standardized tool that provides objective, concrete information with which to evaluate the magnitude of the resident's injury.

Eyes open	**Point value**
Spontaneously	4
To speech	3
To pain	2
No response	1
Verbal response	
Oriented and talking	5
Disoriented/talking	4
Words unintelligible	3
Moaning/groaning	2
No verbalization	1

Monitor response	Point value
Obeys commands	6
Localizes pain	5
Flexion: withdrawal	4
Decorticate: flexion	3
Decerebrate: rigidity	2
No response	1

Scoring the Glasgow coma scale

To score, add the total of all three categories.

Interpretation of results

- A score of less than 8 indicates a neurological crisis
- A score of 9–13 indicates moderate dysfunction
- A score of 13–15 indicates moderate to minor dysfunction

Intake and Output Monitoring as a Nursing Order

Introduction

Intake and output monitoring is a simple nursing procedure that does not require a physician's order. Sadly, nurses sometimes do not take this important intervention seriously, or do not understand the importance of this simple procedure. Many view it as a means of paper compliance, rather than considering how important fluid intake and output is to resident care.

Identify the need for intake and output monitoring, as well as any special approaches or resident preferences on the care plan based on diagnosis, circumstances such as infection, or simply because you suspect something is wrong that we, as nurses can identify and correct. If the resident is known to be at high risk of dehydration upon admission, begin a temporary care plan to address this risk. Because this is a nursing judgment measure, there are no hard, fast, or solid guidelines regarding which residents should be monitored. Any resident at risk for fluid imbalance requires monitoring, either temporarily or permanently. Because the risk is highly variable, identifying specific residents or diagnoses to monitor is highly dependent on accurate nursing assessment and ongoing monitoring, as warranted by resident condition. Keep this in mind when making the determination whether temporary or permanent monitoring is indicated. You also may find that if you initiate an evaluation of intake and output monitoring, nursing assistant staff suddenly becomes attentive to the resident's fluid intake because they know nurses are watching. Hopefully, this attentiveness will persist if you discontinue monitoring after a trial period, but you should always be aware of the possibility that fluid intake may decrease when monitoring is discontinued. The registered dietitian is an excellent resource for you in planning a fluid intake care plan and determining the resident's minimum daily fluid needs. Utilize him or her to assist you in formulating guidelines for monitoring, policies and procedures, and providing education to nursing staff. Generally speaking, facility personnel should routinely monitor fluid balance (intake and output) for:

- all residents receiving tube feedings
- residents with catheters
- residents with urinary tract infection
- residents with physician orders for fluid restrictions or orders to force (encourage) fluids
- resident with specific physician orders for additional liquid (fluid)
- residents who are known to be dehydrated or who are at risk for dehydration
- residents with certain heart and kidney conditions that are at high risk for fluid imbalance
- residents receiving intravenous fluids or parenteral nutrition therapy

Determining fluid needs

The dietitian usually calculates each resident's daily fluid needs on admission and periodically thereafter, based on the resident's weight. He or she uses the following formula, or one similar to it to determine the residents' daily fluid needs:

100 cc/kg for the first 10 kg (22 pounds) of body weight

Add

50 cc/kg for the next 10 kg of body weight

Add

15 cc/kg after the first 20 kg (44 pounds) of body weight

An easy way for nurses to determine the minimum amount of fluid the resident should consume is to estimate 1 cc of fluid for each calorie of dietary intake. Thus, if a resident receives an 1800 calorie diet, he or she requires 1800 cc of fluid in 24 hours. If anything, this is less than many adults require, but it provides a rough estimation. Long term care facility nurses will readily identify that many elderly residents routinely consume less than 1800 cc each day. Ideally, adults should consume 2000 cc to 3000 cc daily, unless fluid restrictions are present. Some require more than this.

Always check the dietary record for your dietitian's calculations for the resident. He or she sees things that affect fluid needs. List the minimum fluid needs on the care plan and develop a plan or care to ensure the resident ingests this amount each day. Monitor I&O to be sure your plan is working and effective.

Need for accurate measurements

The values you document for fluid consumed and excreted are usually estimates, but must be relatively accurate. In other words, you may estimate the fluid intake for a cup of water as being 240cc, when in fact the resident consumed 248cc. Unless the resident has a physician or nursing order for *Strict I&O monitoring*, this estimate is close enough. However, estimating the 240 cc fluid intake as 350cc is not even in the same ballpark. Over the course of a 24 hour day, inaccurate estimates such as this have the potential for markedly changing the fluid balance picture. Make sure your staff can estimate the average amounts for containers used in your facility with reasonable accuracy. Remember that the container measurements may be based on containers that are full to the top. If this is the case, the normal fluid consumption would be *less than* the total measurement for the cup (or other container) that is full to overflowing. Deduct a reasonable amount (usually 15cc to 30cc) to allow the container to be picked up and handled without spillage. Double check your containers to determine whether your guidelines are accurate or need modification. You may want to measure the average fill level on your containers and revise the information on your bedside I&O worksheets, if necessary.

Using the nursing process to evaluate the values

Another important consideration is that monitoring intake and output is *more than recording numbers. In fact, recording numbers is worthless without an accompanying nursing assessment of the meaning of the numbers you document.* Keep this in mind when determining which residents require monitoring, when recording intake throughout the shift, and when documenting the fluid intake and output at the end of each shift. The shift that cumulates the 24 hour totals must also be especially conscientious in adding and evaluating the meaning of the numbers. Failing to add the numbers at the end of the shift or failing to evaluate the totals at the end of each 24 hour period is an unacceptable practice. This is much more than a simple documentation skip because of the potentially devastating outcome on the resident's well-being. Elderly residents have little fluid reserve and can become dehydrated in a surprisingly short period of time. The purpose of this documentation exercise is to use the information to ensure proper care, and we cannot make this assurance if the data are not regularly assessed.

Whomever manages the care plan should make certain to record the dietitian's calculations of each resident's minimum daily fluid needs in a prominent location on the plan. You may also want to document this number on the I&O worksheets and documentation flow sheets. As part of your regular I&O assessment, nurses should compare the fluid consumed with the dietitian's calculations to ensure the resident has taken in at least this minimum amount of fluid each day. If not, adjust the care plan approaches and strive to meet the minimum daily fluid goal for the resident. This must be monitored frequently in some residents. Do not wait for the quarterly care conference!

- Develop an individualized plan of care that takes into account the resident's medical condition, medications, physical problems, catheter, tube feeding, and individual aging changes in hearing, vision, and mobility. Consider the resident's degree of cognitive impairment and ability to consume fluids without help. Communicate the identified risk of fluid imbalance and plan of care to all members of the interdisciplinary team.
- Identify patterns of behavior, individual likes and dislikes leading to fluid imbalance. Develop a plan of care to address these issues to prevent complications.
- Determine what fluids the resident likes and will consume most readily, and attempt to provide these items.
- Promptly meet resident needs. Offer fluids of the resident's choice each time staff are in the room. Place a straw in the resident's mouth and encourage him/her to drink, if necessary. Anticipate needs in cognitively impaired residents who have difficulty communicating.
- Assess for clinical signs and symptoms of fluid imbalance and document the results of this assessment daily, or more often, as indicated. Act immediately to reverse abnormal observations or inadequate fluid intake documented.
- *Nurses must be aware that all tube feeding formulas are approximately 15% solid. Because of this, the resident must have additional free water each shift to prevent dehydration. The formula by itself is never sufficient to meet the resident's bodily*

requirements. Record I&O accurately on residents fed by tube, using a regular I&O record. Do not document the ordered daily amount as given on the regular tube feeding flow sheet. Documentation of this nature is seldom accurate. Intake varies slightly from one day to the next, often due to the amount of water given with medications. It is seldom a fixed amount.

- Routinely record fluid intake and output for residents in whom this is indicated (see above). Total the intake and output records each shift. At the end of 24 hours, the third shift nurse (or nurse designated by facility policy) is responsible for cumulating the daily total. He or she should compare these figures with the resident's minimum body needs. If deficient, pass on the information in report, assess for dehydration, and update the plan of care if indicated. Place the resident in your additional monitoring system for at least 72 hours, or until fluid balance has been restored and is stable. All nursing personnel should take corrective action taken if fluid consumption or urinary output are inadequate. Additional corrective measures may involve changing the plan of care, or obtaining additional consultations.
- Any time a nursing I&O evaluation is ordered, all fluid intake and output will be documented for 3 days, then resident will be assessed for the need for continued monitoring.

Intake and output monitoring

Some nursing personnel are unfamiliar with which fluids to record on the intake and output record. The answer is *all fluids the resident consumes should be recorded.* Follow these guidelines:

- Document all fluid consumed by the resident consumes during each shift in metric measurements (cc or ml) on an intake and output flow sheet or worksheet. This includes fluids consumed on the nursing unit, fluids consumed with medications, fluids consumed during meals, and fluids consumed during activities. (Fluids given with medication pass and during activities are commonly skipped; develop a method for keeping track of them.)

- Record all fluid excreted in metric measurements. For the most part, this is urinary elimination. However, emesis, wound drainage, and liquid stools may also be included in output recording. For incontinent residents, this may be recorded in number of incontinent episodes. For more accurate values (such as when Strict I&O has been ordered), incontinent pads can be weighed to provide an estimate of urinary incontinence fluid output. A metric scale is needed, such as an infant scale. You should post the dry weight of the pads or briefs used by the facility. Any weight above the dry weight is fluid. Use this formula to convert it to milliliters:

  1 gram = 1ml fluid

- At the end of each shift, the nursing assistant assigned to collect the intake and output (I & O) totals the fluid intake and urinary output. These totals are reported to the licensed nurse, who records them in the medical record.
- If, at the end of the shift, the nurse determines that the fluid intake and output are inaccurate or inadequate, he or she should question the assistant(s) about the accuracy of the information and attempt to reconcile the record. He or she may also instruct the nursing assistant to immediately administer additional fluids. Report the low liquid intake to the next shift, who should increase fluid intake and monitor the resident closely.
- Promptly obtain laboratory tests ordered by the physician to assess for the resident's fluid balance, electrolytes, and metabolic status, including hydration.

> *The registered nurse should review the resident's laboratory values relating to hydration.* If abnormal, make phone contact with the physician. Ask the registered dietitian to review the laboratory values and make recommendations. Repeat the laboratory tests periodically to ensure abnormalities have been corrected, or the resident is making improvement. *Simply faxing abnormal lab values to the physician is never appropriate when dehydration is a possibility.* This is reflected early in the blood urea nitrogen (BUN), but other values will become abnormal if the problem is uncorrected. All facility nurses should be able to identify and act on abnormal laboratory values and elevated BUN. Having a resident in a state of mild, chronic dehydration (as reflected by a chronic, low elevation of the BUN) is also unsatisfactory.

Over time, prerenal azotemia develops.

- Develop and implement an individualized plan of care based on the assessment of risk factors and the resident's individual needs.
- If the intake and output/fluid balance goals are not being met, determine whether the care listed in the plan has been or is being provided. Take appropriate corrective action. Consider innovative methods of providing fluids, such as by using popsicles, gelatin, and food products that are high in water. The dietitian can assist you with this issue.

Another significant nursing consideration for evaluating fluid balance is the medications the resident receives. The body uses water as a diluent and vehicle for medications. Drug dosages are calculated based on body weight. *A decrease in total body water will increase the medication concentration per kilogram. Medication toxicity is a real possibility in residents who are dehydrated.* Residents who are dehydrated may experience more medicaion-related side effects. Some medications such as diuretics, laxatives, and others further deplete the body of fluids and increase the risk of dehydration. Use large cups during medication pass. Encourage each resident to consume at least eight ounces of water with medications. Offer juice or other fluids with medication pass, if possible. Document fluid intake, when appropriate.

Discontinuing I&O monitoring

Determining when to discontinue intake and output monitoring also requires the use of good nursing judgment. In general, residents listed on the bulleted list above should be monitored indefinitely. The only exception is those who are being treated for acute urinary tract infections. These residents may be safely discontinued when you are certain the infection has been eliminated (usually 72 hours after the antibiotic is discontinued and/or a subsequent urinalysis shows the infection is no longer present). *However, do not stop monitoring if the fluid intake and output do not reasonably balance.* If this is the case, continue to work on adequate fluid balance and consult the registered dietitian.

Residents who are placed on intake and output as a nursing measure should be reassessed before discontinuing monitoring. Make sure the resident has attained a reasonable intake and output balance for a period of a week to ten days before eliminating I&O monitoring. Even then, consider both a physical assessment and monitoring the BUN and creatinine levels before, and periodically after you discontinue monitoring. If in doubt about the need to continue, consult the registered dietitian. Note the resident's high risk status in a prominent location on the care plan and other records, as appropriate.

Always remember that dehydration can pose serious problems in the long term care population. Many residents may have subclinical dehydration, but the condition is so subtle that it is not recognized or identified unless a blood test is done. Even then, slightly abnormal values may be considered insignificant by an untrained reviewer. Intake and output monitoring should be viewed as an important, therapeutic nursing measure. Always err on the side of caution and resident safety. Avoid viewing I&O as a "make work" or "paper compliance" activity. Accurately performing this simple procedure is important to resident safety, well-being, and good health

Mental and consciousness evaluation

The resident's level of consciousness and mental orientation are important indicators of neurological status. A change in level of conscious is the most important sign of neurologic deterioration.

To assess level of consciousness and orientation,

- ask the resident his or her name. If the resident responds correctly, evaluate response to date/time, place, and situation. If response is appropriate, ask about season and year.
  - Disorientation commonly affects the resident's knowledge of date first, followed by time, place, caregiver, and self.
- assess the quality of the verbal response. Evaluate the clarity of the resident's speech and his or her ability to make him- or herself understood. Rambling responses suggest the resident is having problems with thought processes and organization.
- evaluate the resident's ability to follow directions. Determine whether he or she can follow a simple command. Evaluate the resident's ability to remain focused on the task.
- try painful stimuli if the resident does not respond to verbal stimuli. Assess for a response on both sides of the body to rule out monoplegia (paralysis of one limb).

To evaluate motor function,

- test the resident's grip strength using both hands simultaneously. Instruct him or her to squeeze your fingers as hard as possible. Compare the grip strength in both hands. The dominant hand may be slightly stronger.
- instruct the resident to close his or her eyes and extend the arms forward. Position the palms facing upward. Determine whether either arm falls downward or pronates, indicating muscle weakness.
- apply gentle downward pressure to the resident's leg. Instruct the resident to raise the leg while you press gently downward. Press gently on the midthigh to evaluate muscle strength.
- in an unconscious resident, apply painful stimulus. With a pencil or pen, press on the fingernail bed. If the resident withdraws, compare the strength of each arm.

  Note: If decorticate (figure 5.1a) or decerebrate (figure 5.1b) posturing develops in response to painful stimuli, discontinue the assessment and immediately notify the physician. If the physician does not respond immediately, send the resident to the emergency department using a 911 emergency ambulance. Do not call a transfer service.

Figure 5.1a

Decorticate posture is a sign of severe neurologic problems. It is an exaggerated posture of upper extremity flexion and abduction accompanied by rigid lower extremity extension in response to external stimuli. This position is an ominous sign, and indicates the resident requires prompt transfer to an acute care hospital.

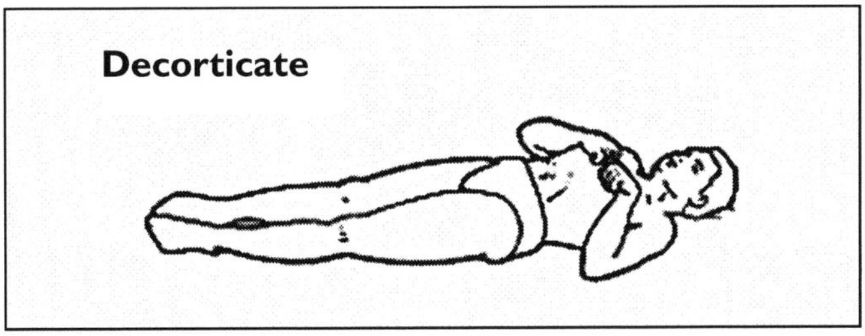

Figure 5.1b

Decerebrate rigidity is an exaggerated position of extension resulting from a lesion of the brain stem. It is manifested as a posture of lying in rigid extension with arms internally rotated at the shoulders and pronated. The elbows, knees, and hips are rigidly extended, with the fingers, ankles, and toes flexed. This position is an ominous sign, and indicates the resident requires prompt transfer to an acute care hospital.

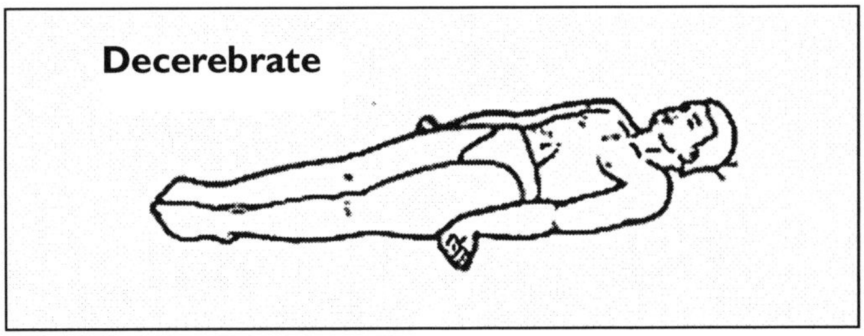

- manually flex and extend the extremities to evaluate muscle tone.
- stroke the lateral foot with your thumbnail to evaluate the plantar reflex. The toes should flex. Observe for a positive Babinski sign, suggesting an upper motor neuron lesion. (A positive Babinski sign is extension of the great toe and abduction of the other toes instead of the normal flexion reflex).
- Complete the neurological assessment by checking vital signs and pupils and completing the Glasgow Coma Scale.

Neurologic checks, example policy and procedure for

The standard of long-term care nursing practice requires monitoring of residents with known or suspected head injury for a minimum of 72 hours, and longer or as needed if symptoms are present. The frequency of monitoring is intense. Although the tests are repetitious, they will promptly identify significant changes in the resident's condition. Immediately after the injury, monitor neurologic checks every 15 minutes. If the resident is stable, you can safely increase the time frame.

Over a 24-hour period, the frequency of monitoring decreases to every four to eight hours, depending on resident condition, physician orders, and facility policy. At a minimum, monitoring should include the following:

- Assessing the resident for changes in level of consciousness, which is a cardinal sign of untoward pathology. Assess the resident immediately after the fall, then frequently throughout the shift. Continue monitoring for a minimum of 72 hours, or until resolution of the incident. Let your findings guide your assessment. Inform the physician promptly if abnormalities develop. The assessment should include, at a minimum, pulse, respiration, and blood pressure measurements; assessment of pupil size and reactivity; and equality of hand grasps. Most facilities have a neurological check sheet that specifies assessments to be done. Everything listed is important. Do not pick and choose which assessments to complete.
- Observing the resident for a minimum of 72 hours for
    - obvious injuries to the scalp, including lacerations, bruises, or contusions

- confusion
- memory loss
- difficulty speaking
- gait or balance problems
- pupils of unequal size or reaction
- headache
- vomiting
- visual disturbances
- periods of coherence alternating with periods of confusion or lethargy

• Completing the Glasgow Coma Scale immediately, then once each shift.

• Making a complete neurologic assessment, including vital signs upon occurrence, then checking neurologic signs, including at least

- assessment of pupil size and reactivity
- equality of hand grasps
- pulse, respiration, and blood pressure

• If the resident is stable, progress monitoring to every 30 minutes for two hours.

• If the resident remains stable, increase monitoring to every 60 minutes for two hours.

• If the resident remains stable, progress to every four hours for 24 hours.

• If the resident continues to be stable, progress monitoring to every eight hours (once a shift) until 72 hours has elapsed.

After the initial assessment, inform the physician of your findings and document his or her response and new orders. Prepare the resident for a CT scan, x-rays, or other diagnostic tests as ordered. You should also do the following:

- Notify the responsible party of the fall or other injury.
- Administer mild analgesic medications as ordered.
- Update the care plan to reflect special monitoring related to the head injury. Make sure all staff on your shift are aware of the head injury. Report the incident to the oncoming shift.
- Document the incident, monitoring, notifications, and other information according to facility policy.

Other nursing care that may be appropriate includes the following:

- Initially after the head injury, elevating the resident's head to reduce intracranial pressure.
- Minimizing resident movement.
- Keeping the environment subdued. A nursing goal during the initial post-injury period is to keep the resident calm and stress free.
- Monitoring fluid intake and output.
- Monitoring the resident's appetite.
- Ensuring that the resident is assisted with meals and fluid consumption, if needed.
- Ensuring that the resident is regularly turned and properly positioned, if bedfast during this period of time.

- Implementing safety measures to ensure that the resident will not fall out of bed, as appropriate.
- Documenting nursing observations and the resident's response to care provided.
- After the acute phase has passed, assessing the cause of the resident's fall and taking measures to prevent recurrence; describe these measures on the care plan.

Neurological checks

Neurological (neuro) checks are performed when a neurological disorder or injury is suspected. Neuro checks are normally documented on a flow sheet. The following points are essential to a thorough assessment. Avoid documenting, "Neuro's negative." List each component of the assessment individually and note the results.

Level of consciousness

The level of consciousness is always the most important indicator of cerebral injury or other neurological problem. Apply the following definitions consistently when describing the resident:

- Alert: The resident is awake and responds appropriately
- Lethargic: The resident is very sleepy, but arouses to stimulation
- Obtunded: The resident is difficult to arouse, but responds appropriately
- Stuporous: The resident is not completely alert, but responds to pain
- Semicomatose: The resident has reflex movements and responds to pain
- Comatose: The resident is completely unresponsive to stimuli

Orientation

Orientation is a measurement of the resident's awareness to

- person
- place

- time
- situation

Judgment

Judgment is the ability to discern, evaluate, and form opinions. Evaluate whether the resident:

- expresses coherent thoughts
- expresses distorted thoughts
- formulates an appropriate verbal response

Memory

Memory is the ability to recall what is experienced, learned, or retained. Evaluate the resident's ability to remember using the following:

- Short term: Short-term memory is the primary or active memory. It stores a limited amount of information for a limited amount of time. Some experts state that no more than seven items can be stored in the short-term memory.
- Past: The past memory is the result of recent mental processing. It may be called the working memory.
- Long term: Long-term memory stores an unlimited amount of information indefinitely. It can be described as the capacity (or capacities) to retain information in an active, highly available state.

Affect

Affect is the emotional tone, feeling, or mood attached to a thought, including its external manifestations. During neurological evaluation, affect may be described as being

- alert
- pleasant
- restricted
- dull or blunt

Speech

The resident's ability to speak at will is described as one of the following:

- Aphasia: inability to speak
- Dysphasia: difficulty speaking
- Articulate: speaks fluently
- Appropriate/inappropriate

Pain

The response to pain is a measure of the resident's response to external stimulation:

- Reaction to stimulation: The resident's reaction to verbal stimuli, touch, smell, or other stimuli
- Reaction to painful stimulation: The resident's reaction to painful stimuli, such as a sternal rub or pressing on the nail bed with a pen

Pupil assessment

Early assessment of pupil size and response (figure 5.2) to light is critical for establishing a baseline measurement. Continue to monitor and compare the pupil response during subsequent neurologic checks. Increased intracranial pressure or temporal lobe herniation will cause pupil dilation. This almost always develops on the side of increased pressure. Initially, the pupil on the same side is reactive to light. It subsequently becomes sluggish, then fails to respond to light at all. As the intracranial pressure increases, the pupil on the opposite side is similarly affected. Determine whether pupils are:

- equal
- reactive/nonreactive
- sluggish

Motor response

This is the best response to motor stimulation. Examine all four extremities. Inform the physician immediately if the resident becomes

- decorticate: a unilateral or bilateral postural change; arms are flexed and adducted and legs are involuntarily positioned in rigid extension (also refer to figure 5.1a)
- decerebrate: a postural change consisting of episodes of opisthotonos (spasticity in which the spine and extremities are bent forward, the body resting on the head and the heels), rigid extension of the arms and legs, internal rotation of the arms, and marked plantar flexion of the feet (also refer to figure 5.1b)

Figure 5.2

Early assessment of pupil size, response to light, and accommodation are critical to establish a baseline measurement of the resident's status. Ongoing monitoring is essential during neurologic checks. Increased intracranial pressure or temporal lobe herniation will cause pupil dilation on the side of increased pressure.

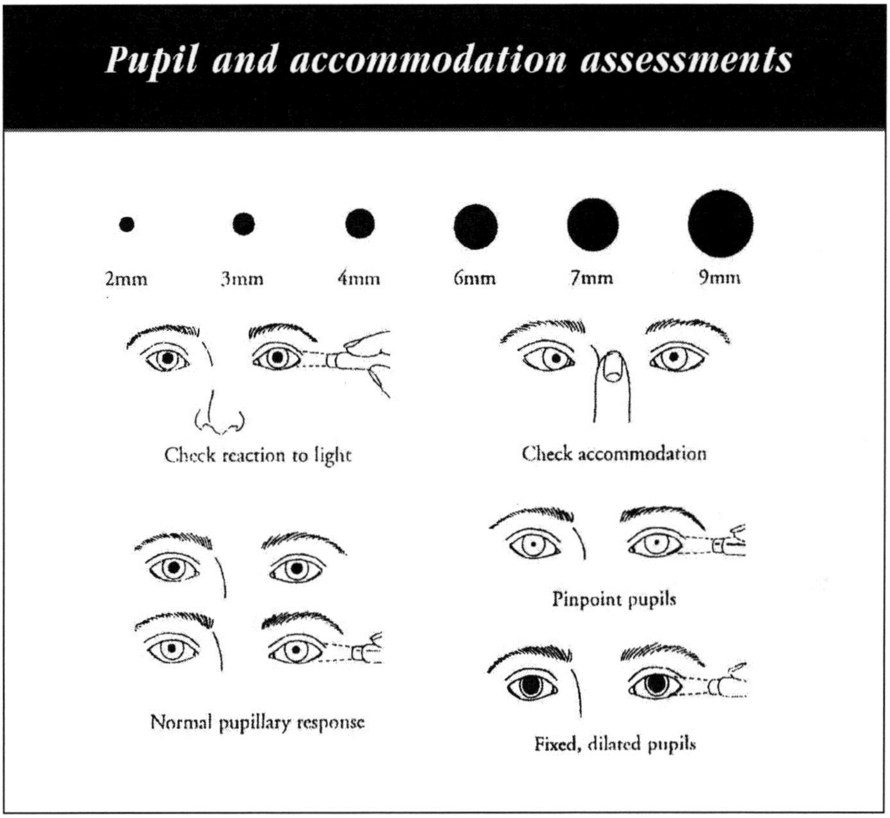

Pupil assessment

To conduct a pupil assessment, take the following steps:

1. Dim the lights.
2. Ask the resident to look at an object or location straight across the room:
   - Under these conditions, the pupils will spontaneously dilate (normal response)
3. Use a penlight, if possible. Remind the resident to continue looking straight ahead. Turn on the light and move it from one side of the head to the eye:
   - The pupil will constrict quickly (normal response)
4. Allow the resident to blink to lubricate eye (prevents discomfort).
5. Repeat procedure with the other eye.
6. Compare the reactions of both eyes. Both pupils should constrict equally.
7. Ask the resident to look at an object or location across the room.
8. Hold one finger about 4 inches from the resident's nose.
9. Instruct the resident to focus on your finger. Slowly move it closer to his or her nose:
   - Eyes will converge on your finger and the pupils will constrict (normal accommodation)

- Note:
  - Know the resident's ocular history; be aware of the presence of an artificial eye.
  - Up to 15% of all adults have a measurable difference in pupil size.
  - In serious medical problems, a resident with an abnormal pupil will most probably have additional neurologic signs and symptoms to assist in confirming the diagnosis (e.g., stupor, nerve palsies, droopy lid, loss of vision, etc.). If the only problem is uneven pupils, then the most likely cause is typically not life-threatening.

Developmental considerations

- Pupil size decreases with age
- The lens loses elasticity with age
- Visual acuity often decreases with age
- Elderly persons have an increased risk of glaucoma and cataracts

Documentation

- Date, time, pupil size, shape, and reaction
- Normal pupils are 3 mm–5 mm in diameter and respond equally to light
- *Always document pupil size in millimeters*
- Note abnormalities, and take appropriate nursing action

Other documentation considerations

PERRLA

- **P**: Pupils
- **E**: Equal
- **R**: Round
- **R**: Reactive
- **L**: Light
- **A**: Accommodation (adaptation of the eye for near vision; you evaluate this when the pupil dilates as the resident focuses on a distant object, then converges and constricts with a near object)

Eye abnormalities

- **Anisocoria:** a condition in which one pupil is larger than the other.
- **Conjunctivitis:** inflammation of the conjunctiva. Eyes may appear red; drainage suggests infection.
- **Hyperopia:** Farsightedness; light rays focus behind the retina.
- **Myopia:** Nearsightedness; light focuses in front of the retina.
- **Nonreactive pupils:** fixed in midposition and do not react. They may be slightly ovoid or irregularly shaped. This is an indication of midbrain swelling or lesions.
- **Periorbital edema:** edema of the eyelid; a collection of excess fluid.
- **Pinpoint pupils:** smaller than 2 mm in diameter. They indicate a lesion or compression of the pons in the brain stem.
- **Photophobia:** light-induced pain; abnormal sensitivity to light (the amount of light entering the eye); usually, the iris is unable to constrict enough to reduce the light entering the eye.
- **Presbyopia:** the decreased ability of the eye to change shape in order to accommodate to near vision.
- **Ptosis:** drooping or lagging of an eyelid.
- **Sclera icterus:** jaundice in the eye; a yellowish discoloration of the sclera.

- **Fixed, dilated pupils:** indicate medullary dysfunction, which may occur with intracranial swelling or bleeding, CVA, profound hypoxia, or brain death. Other potential causes of dilated pupils include the following:
  - Anticholinergic drugs
  - Certain eyedrops
  - Imitrex, phenylephrine, Wellbutrin, atropine
  - Illicit (street) drugs
  - Medication overdose (type of an adverse drug reaction)
  - Brain injury
  - Stroke
  - Brain tumor
- **Pupil constriction:** reduction in pupil size. This is a normal reaction to light. Other potential causes of constricted pupils are
  - opioids and some eyedrops. *Examples:* Opium and derivatives: codeine, morphine, heroin. Synthetics: methadone, meperidine (Demerol), hydromorphone (Dilaudid), oxycodone (Percodan), pentazocine (Talwin-Nx). (Note: some of these drugs are not recommended for use in elderly persons, but are listed here because many long-term care facilities also accept young and middle-aged adult residents.)
  - iritis: inflammation of the iris.

Other diseases and conditions that may affect pupil size and reaction

- Multiple sclerosis
- Brain tumor
- Syphilis

Nursing diagnoses associated with visual disorders

- Sensory/perceptual alteration: visual
- Impaired home maintenance management
- Pain related to inflammation
- Self-esteem disturbance

Section VI:

Resources

Standardized code words[1]

The following code words are recommended for standardization and have been adopted by a number of hospitals and long-term care facilities.

- Code Red: fire
- Code Blue: medical emergency—adult
- Code White: medical emergency—pediatric
- Code Pink: infant abduction
- Code Purple: child abduction
- Code Yellow: bomb threat
- Code Gray: combative person
- Code Silver: person with a weapon/hostage situation
- Code Orange: hazardous material spill/release
- Code Triage Internal: an internal disaster
- Code Triage External: an external disaster

Note: This list was originally developed for acute care, and there is no code word for resident elopement. Facilities using this list should consider adding this code to the list by using "code brown" or another term that has not been designated above. Be aware that other healthcare workers, such as physicians and EMS, may be in your facility when a code is called. Avoid confusion—do not change the designation of the colors listed above.

1. Adams, C. 2000. In wake of tragedy, California adopts universal hospital emergency codes. *Access Control and Security Systems*. Nov 1 2000. Online. *http://securitysolutions.com/mag/security_wake_tragedy_california/index.html*.

Types and causes of stroke

Type of stroke	Cause
Ischemic	The most common type of stroke; accounts for approximately 80% of all strokes. Caused by a clot or other blockage within an artery leading to the brain.
Embolic	A clot develops in a part of the body other than the brain (commonly the heart). It travels through the bloodstream into the brain, where it lodges in a small artery. This stroke occurs suddenly and without warning. Approximately 15% percent of embolic strokes occur in people with atrial fibrillation.
Thrombotic	A clot forms in the blood vessels of the brain; usually one of the cerebral arteries. It remains attached to the artery wall until it grows large enough to occlude blood flow. May be preceded by one or more TIAs.
Lacunar infarct	These are small, deep infarcts located mainly in the basal ganglia and thalamus that may also affect the brain stem, internal and external capsules, and periventricular white matter. When a stroke occurs due to small-vessel disease, a small infarction results, sometimes called a lacunar infarction. Most likely caused by atherosclerotic occlusion of perforating branches, lacunar infarcts account for approximately 25% of all ischemic strokes. *Lacunar* comes from the Latin word meaning "hole" or "cavity." Lacunar infarctions commonly occur in persons with diabetes or hypertension.

Type of stroke	Cause
Cerebral hemorrhage	Caused by the sudden rupture of an artery in the brain; during a cerebral hemorhage blood spills out, compressing brain structures. Approximately 20% of strokes are caused by hemorrhage.
Subarachnoid hemorrhage	Caused by the sudden rupture of an artery; the location of the rupture leads to blood filling the space surrounding the brain rather than inside of it.

Characteristics of right and left hemiparesis

Hemiparesis	Characteristics (residents may have some but not all of these)
Right hemiparesis	• Aphasia/speech impairment • Hearing impairment • Writing impairment • Impaired ability for abstract thinking • Difficulty recalling symbols • Impaired ability to understand what he or she hears
Left hemiparesis	• Loss of speech inhibition, uncontrolled talking • Memory problems • Unilateral neglect • Loss of numerical concept (important if numeric pain scale is used) • Limited awareness of errors • Although resident is able to communicate, may be more disabled than residents with right hemiplegia

Hemiparesis	Characteristics (residents may have some but not all of these)
Right or left hemiparesis	• Emotional lability, may laugh or cry inappropriately • Loss of sensation on affected side • Loss of three-dimensional concepts; cannot identify objects by feel • Loss of sense of position of extremities • Easily fatigued • Paralysis; usually flaccid, but may be spastic • Impaired sense of balance • Pain in arm and shoulder

Hip precautions

List hip precautions on the care plan and instruct staff in care of the resident. Hip precautions are usually maintained for the first six weeks after surgery, or as ordered by the physician. Hip precautions commonly entail the following:

- Avoid
  - extreme bending at the hip
  - crossing the legs
  - acute flexion of the hips and legs (the therapist will give directions for positioning and the degree of flexion permitted, but generally, the resident should never flex the hip more than 90°)
- Never elevate the head of the bed more than 45°
- Attach a trapeze to the bed to assist with movement
- Instruct the resident to avoid pressing down on the foot of the affected leg when using the trapeze or moving in bed
- Provide a fracture bedpan, if needed when in bed
- Use an elevated toilet seat when out of bed
- Avoid positioning on the abdomen
- Avoid positioning on the operative side
- Use an abduction pillow or position regular foam pillows between the legs when positioned on the back or unaffected side

- Position the operative leg in good alignment at all times
- Avoid low chairs or couches; position only in chairs with arms in which the knees remain lower than the hips, and avoid positions in which the knees are higher than the hips
- Avoid leaning forward while sitting
- Avoid flexing the hips more than 90° or internally or externally rotating the foot and leg
- Avoid bending over to pick up objects from the floor or put on socks and shoes
- Remove staples two to three weeks after surgery
- Keep the incision open to air unless infection present or physician's order to cover
- The resident may shower five to seven days after surgery; pat the incision dry; avoid creams or lotions
- Apply antiembolism hosiery and have the resident wear 24 hours a day or as ordered; remove every four hours for circulation check and for bathing; wear hosiery for four to six weeks
- Avoid sitting for more than 30–45 minutes at a time
- Provide range of motion exercises on the unaffected extremities
- Assist with turning and repositioning as needed
- Assist with coughing and deep breathing exercises if the resident is bedfast
- Provide aggressive pressure ulcer prevention measures

Suicide precautions

Suicide precautions

Example policy and procedure for suicide precautions

If a resident states he or she no longer wishes to live and intends to harm him- or herself, the facility will initiate suicide precautions. This includes, in some circumstances, modifying the physical environment and securing the assistance of mental health professionals when an unusual potential for injury is the result of the expressed wishes of a resident. The facility will maintain such procedures and modify them as necessary in specific circumstances.

Policy interpretation and implementation

When the resident communicates a desire to commit suicide, staff should:

1. Licensed nurse:

    - request a social service consultation
    - notify the attending physician
    - request an order for a psychological consultation
    - update the care plan and communicate the resident's intention to other staff, as appropriate
    - review the MDS to determine whether a significant change assessment is necessary
    - schedule the resident for review during the next care plan meeting
    - notify the responsible party

2. Maintain a one-on-one relationship with the resident. Do not leave the resident alone when actively suicidal.

3. If the resident is in immediate danger to self or others, the facility will proceed with a 911 emergency transfer to the acute care psychiatric unit.

4. Search the resident's room thoroughly each shift for any and all potentially dangerous objects, including chemicals. Look inside containers and between folded clothing. Check pockets of clothing in closets and drawers. Remove all potentially harmful items from the room and the resident's person. Also take the following measures:

    - Remove call signal (cord) and replace with hand bell
    - Remove sharp objects, all objects with cords, belts, medications, and other potentially harmful items
    - Remove all plastic bags from room
    - Instruct dietary staff to provide all meals with disposable dishes, trays, glasses, and utensils
    - Check the food tray promptly after each meal to ensure utensils are present
    - Bag and label all confiscated items with the resident's name and give to social worker for safekeeping or disposition
    - Once initiated, suicide precautions will remain in place for a minimum of 72 hours and then be reevaluated

5. Notify the facility administrator, director of nursing, and nursing supervisor of the resident changes and the initiation of suicide precautions.

6. Check on resident every 15 minutes to ensure resident's safety. Simply "looking in" to be sure the resident is safe is sufficient. Document these checks on a daily flow sheet. Staff will report no less than hourly and report any observed behavior changes to the nurse in charge. Increase the frequency of monitoring at the nurse's discretion. Document the results.

7. The nurse will chart behaviors in the nursing notes each shift and reassess as needed.

8. Nursing and social services will document observations, efforts, interventions, and resident response in progress notes.

9. Advise the attending physician of recommendations made by mental health professional.

10. End safety precautions when the interdisciplinary team, mental health consultant, social worker, and attending physician concur that they are no longer necessary:

    - Secure a physicians' order to terminate the precautions

11. If suicide precautions are initiated for any resident, the interventions will be reviewed during the next quality assurance meeting.

Prerenal azotemia and acute renal failure

Prerenal azotemia is the most common form of kidney failure seen in hospitalized patients. Long-term care facility residents who are hospitalized are commonly diagnosed with prerenal azotemia, particularly if they have been diagnosed with dehydration. Occasionally, a resident will be diagnosed with acute renal failure (ARF), despite having no known history of renal disease. Prerenal azotemia causes about 50%–80% of all ARF cases. Inadequate perfusion of the kidneys occurs as a result of extracellular fluid volume depletion or cardiovascular disease.

Fluid needs

The average adult requires a minimum of 1,375 mL of fluid each day to maintain proper kidney function. Prerenal azotemia occurs as a result of reduced blood flow to the kidneys. The kidneys filter the blood as it is forced under pressure through the glomeruli. When the circulating volume or pressure of the blood flow through the kidneys is reduced, they do not function properly. Glomerular filtration is markedly decreased, or may not occur at all. Since urine output is reduced, waste products accumulate in the bloodstream. The kidneys (glomeruli and tubules) continue to do their jobs by filtering wastes. However, without sufficient fluid, the rate of filtration is so slow that many wastes are reabsorbed into the blood, instead of being excreted in the urine.

Common causes

The buildup of nitrogen waste products and accumulation of excess fluid in the body are responsible for most of the symptoms of prerenal azotemia and acute renal failure.

Common causes of this condition are

- dehydration (most common cause)
- conditions in which the heart cannot pump sufficient blood (or blood is pumped at low volume)
- heart failure
- vomiting
- diarrhea
- bleeding
- burns

Less common causes are

- shock, including septic shock
- trauma to the kidneys
- renal artery embolism or occlusion
- some surgeries

Signs and symptoms

Signs and symptoms of prerenal azotemia include

- reduced urine production; little or no urine produced
- confusion, decreased alertness, progressively worsening
- pallor
- rapid pulse
- dry mouth

- thirst
- edema
- abdominal pain
- may have increased urination at night
- the resident may have signs or symptoms of infection elsewhere in the body

Late signs and symptoms include

- low blood pressure
- signs of shock
- decreased pulse pressure

Diagnosis

The condition is diagnosed through electrolyte monitoring. CBC and urinalysis are also routinely done. Urea is a small molecule, whereas creatinine is larger. In prerenal azotemia, levels of urea rise faster than the levels of creatinine. Because of their size, urea molecules more readily return to the bloodstream when glomerular filtration is slow. Creatinine is excreted, but its excretion is less than normal. Laboratory tests reveal an accumulation of nitrogen wastes, such as urea and creatinine in the blood. This is called azotemia. Other waste products accumulate and act as toxins, causing tissue damage and interfering with organ function throughout the body. A buildup of nitrogenous wastes and accumulation of fluid causes symptoms of prerenal azotemia. Laboratory testing reveals the following:

- Elevated BUN
- Elevated creatinine
- Increased BUN/creatinine ratio

- Gradual serum potassium increase
- Low urine sodium
- High urine creatinine to serum creatinine ratio
- Increased osmolality and specific gravity of urine

Prevention

This a serious condition that can cause permanent renal damage and failure. Being aware of the resident's risk factors, prevention of dehydration, and close monitoring are always best. Regularly monitor the at-risk resident's laboratory values. Other nursing measures include

- monitoring intake and output; never hesitate to order I&O as a nursing measure
- carefully *evaluating* fluid intake and output every 24 hours and comparing with dietitian's recommended fluid needs
- monitoring weight
- monitoring vital signs
- monitoring level of consciousness
- encouraging fluids

Treatment

The primary treatment goal is to correct the cause as quickly as possible to prevent permanent kidney damage. The resident is usually hospitalized and may be admitted to the intensive care unit. Treatment often includes hemodialysis or peritoneal dialysis. The resident will be given IV fluids to increase and restore blood volume. Drugs are used to increase cardiac output.

Prerenal azotemia is reversible if the cause is promptly identified and corrected within 24 hours of onset of the condition. If it progresses undetected, acute tubular necrosis, acute renal failure, and internal renal damage will occur. As you can see, this condition is preventable with proper nursing monitoring and care, as well as attentiveness to fluid intake and output.

Standard of care for monitoring residents with acute illness or infection

Nurses and paraprofessional nursing personnel are responsible for regular, ongoing monitoring of residents who have experienced an acute illness, infection, incident, or other event. Any change in condition, no matter how minor, falls into this category. The resident must be monitored for as long as necessary to ensure that the event is resolved and that the resident's condition has been stabilized. Most facilities monitor the resident for the abnormal condition every shift until 24 hours after he or she is stabilized and the illness or event resolved. If abnormal observations are noted, the licensed nurse must take the appropriate nursing action, providing the necessary interventions and notifications. If a resident experiences a change in condition, nursing personnel should take the following steps:

1. Monitor the resident regularly on all shifts until at least 24 hours after the acute event is completely resolved. Monitoring may continue for days or weeks, depending on the nature of the precipitating occurrence and the resident's response.

2. Monitor vital signs (temperature, pulse, respirations, and blood pressure) at least once every eight-hour shift. Check vital signs more frequently if one or more of the values are abnormal, or the resident's condition warrants it.

3. Conduct a focused assessment of the resident's systems, based on the nature of his or her problem, at least once each shift. For example, for a resident with upper respiratory infection, the nurse should assess and document

- auscultation of lung sounds. Assess the nature of sounds and adequacy of chest expansion, rate, rhythm, depth of respirations, and use of accessory respiratory muscles.
- color of the resident's skin, lips, and fingernail beds.
- change in mental status or level of consciousness.
- increased restlessness.
- shortness of breath or other difficulty breathing.
- presence or absence of cough; if present, note whether it is productive or nonproductive, with color, character, and amount of secretions.
- presence or absence of signs and symptoms related to the specific infection. For example, note the presence or absence of nasal drainage.

4. Report results of monitoring to the oncoming nurse in the change of shift report.
5. Notify the physician immediately if abnormalities are noted.
6. Inform the responsible party of the change and action taken.
7. Update the care plan to reflect the additional observations and monitoring and care required because of the acute illness, infection, change in condition, or abnormal observation.
8. Document the results of monitoring, observations, nursing interventions, notifications, and the resident's response in the nurses' notes. If the resident is on antibiotics or other therapy, document the condition for which the antibiotics are being given. Avoid entries such as "no side effects to antibiotics." This is an appropriate entry in addition to other information, but the

absence of side effects can be easily noted on the medication record or flow sheet. Your nursing notes should address your assessment of the acute medical problem or injury and actions taken, as noted above.

9. If the resident is not responding to treatment for an acute medical problem, contact the physician.